"And Then Freddie Told Tiger..."

"And Then Freddie Told Tiger..."

A Collection of the Best True Golf Stories of All Time

DON WADE
Foreword by Amy Alcott

CB
CONTEMPORARY BOOKS

Library of Congress Cataloging-in-Publication Data

Wade, Don.
    "And then Freddie told Tiger . . ." : a collection of the best true
golf stories of all time / Don Wade ; illustrations by Paul Szep.
      p.   cm.
    ISBN 0-8092-3007-0
    1. Golf—Anecdotes.   I. Title.
GV967.W269   1998
796.352—dc21

                                                 98-9846
                                                   CIP

Illustrations by Paul Szep

Published by Contemporary Books
A division of NTC/Contemporary Publishing Group, Inc.
4255 West Touhy Avenue, Lincolnwood (Chicago), Illinois 60646-1975 U.S.A.
Copyright © 1998 by Don Wade
Printed in the United States of America
International Standard Book Number: 0-8092-3007-0

98 99 00 01 02 03 QP 17 16 15 14 13 12 11 10 9 8 7 6 5 4 3 2

*To all the people who have shared
their stories and their friendship*

CONTENTS

FOREWORD

It doesn't seem possible, but Don Wade and I have been friends for twenty years. We met on a beautiful New England summer day in 1979. I had just finished a practice round for the U.S. Women's Open at Brooklawn Country Club in Fairfield, Connecticut. Don was an editor at *Golf Digest* and was working on a story about the LPGA Tour. What was supposed to be a quick interview lasted through one of the funniest lunches I've ever had, and a great friendship was born.

Over the years, Don and I have collaborated on a book, a video, and more magazine articles than I can count. But more important than all that, we've been there for each other in all the good times and bad times that life can throw at you.

Some of the happiest hours we've shared have been at dinners where we've traded stories about the people and places that are such a big part of the game. Some are wickedly funny. Some would be just too weird to believe—if they weren't about golf. Others are so sad they'll bring a tear to your eye.

When Don's first collection of anecdotes, *"And Then Jack Said to Arnie . . ."*, came out in 1991, I knew it would be a bestseller. After all, the book was like being there at one of our dinners. The same is true for all the books that have fol-

lowed in the series. I love these books, and I'm glad so many of the stories I've shared with Don are in them.

I know you'll love this book too. It's like having dinner with two old friends who are crazy about golf—and each other.

Amy Alcott

PREFACE

Those of you who have read this series of books will notice that certain people are quoted more than others. Some are friends whom I've done books with over the years, such as Sam Snead and Ken Venturi, Amy Alcott and Nancy Lopez. Some are in television, like Frank Chirkinian and Jim Nantz and Gary McCord. Others are writers who were willing to share stories they collected over long and charmed lives, guys like Bob Drum, Charlie Price, and Dick Taylor—all of whom have now passed on.

The one thing all of these people had in common was that they were "Golf Guys," who loved the people and places and history of the game and were somehow blessed enough to carve out a livelihood in golf.

Dave Marr, who died in 1997, was the ultimate Golf Guy, and I think he'd like to be remembered that way. He learned the game from his father, who was a professional, and from the likes of Claude Harmon, Ben Hogan, and Jimmy Demaret. He learned his lessons well enough to win the 1965 PGA Championship.

Demaret also gave him valuable lessons on how to deal with writers.

"When I first came out on tour I traveled with Jimmy for a while," Dave once told me. "We'd go into these towns where the writers didn't know anything about golf or the guys on tour. Jimmy would sit with them for hours and give them stories they could use. I was always struck that he would take the time to do that."

Over the years, Dave Marr was a great source. He might tip you off to a good story, or steer you away from a bad one. He was a guy you always looked forward to seeing at a tournament, both at the course and away from it at night when the real business of journalism is done. He was especially good at introducing young writers around. They were his "cubs," as in cub reporters, and a lot of us owe a lot to him.

Conversely, he went out of his way to talk to young players and give them advice about how important a good relationship with the press can be to a player's career. In March, just a few months before he died, I spent some time with Dave at The Players Championship. At that time a very good player, Scott Hoch, had decided he had been burned by the press and was no longer going to grace writers with his insights.

It should be noted that this didn't appear to bother many of the writers.

It did, however, bother Dave Marr, who thought it was one of the single dumbest things he'd ever seen. It is a measure of the man that, even though he was wasting away from the cancer that would soon kill him, he planned to have a quiet talk with Hoch. I don't know if he ever did. I do know that a short while later, Hoch called off his boycott.

Early in his career, Dave Marr had been an assistant pro at Winged Foot, and it was an experience he treasured. He once described the place as "the ultimate golf club."

"Golf is a game of honor at Winged Foot, and that's ingrained in everyone," he said. "The members always try to shoot the best score, play it as it lies, and count every stroke. Then you go to the grillroom and tell stories and lies. It's a perfect place."

Spoken like a true Golf Guy about the game he truly loved.

ACKNOWLEDGMENTS

This is the sixth book in a series that began in 1991 with the publication of *"And Then Jack Said to Arnie . . ."*. Among the many people who deserve thanks and credit are the players, writers, television guys, and golf fans who have been so generous and so willing to share their stories.

There are some people who have been involved with these books from the beginning, and to the extent that the series has been successful, these people deserve credit.

Paul Szep, who has done all the illustrations for these books, has two Pulitzer Prizes to show for his efforts as an editorial cartoonist for the *Boston Globe*. I know this is true, but while I've been to his house dozens of times, I've never actually seen them. I suspect this is because he keeps them in a room with his other most prized possessions—the bags of golf clubs, golf shoes, golf magazines, and trophies that serve as a cluttered testimonial to his passionate love affair with the game. It's a love that's reflected in the drawings that grace these books, and I thank him.

Steve Szurlej, who has shot the covers for each of these books, is the senior staff photographer for *Golf Digest* and one of the most professional people in his business. I've seen him at work in the early-morning solitude of a golf course as he patiently waited for just the right light to capture the true beauty of a golf hole. I've seen him elbow his way through the crush of photographers at Major championships so he could be in just the right place to capture history. In shooting the covers for these books, he has also captured the spirit of friendship and camaraderie that is at the heart of the game, and for that I thank him too.

Nancy Crossman was the editor who believed in these books right from the start and was tireless in her nurturing and support, as well as her friendship. When she decided to leave corporate life and strike out on her own earlier this year, I was handed off to senior editor Matthew Carnicelli. Early in his career, he had worked on one of my books for another publisher. In spite of this, he agreed to take on this burden, and he has done so with patience, skill, and good humor. I look forward to working with him for many years—and books—to come.

When you decide to try to make a go of it as a writer, no one is more important than your agent. You need someone who believes in you and your talent. You need someone who is candid and honest, tough and fair, bright and funny. Thank you, Chris Tomasino, for being all those things for all these years.

And when you decide to make a go of it as a writer, you'd better have a family that believes in you and trusts in the future, whatever that may hold. Thank you, Julia, for that. And thanks to our kids, Ben, Darcy, and Andy, too.

"He'll feel much better if he reads
'And Then Freddie Told Tiger . . .'"

"And Then Freddie Told Tiger..."

ARCHITECTS

Architect A. W. Tillinghast came from a wealthy and well-connected society family. He could be imperious at times, was known to take a drink, and had a certain roguish quality about him. On top of these laudable qualities, he was positively a genius when it came to designing golf courses, having created masterpieces like the two courses at Winged Foot and at neighboring Quaker Ridge.

It's not surprising, then, that when his daughter brought a boyfriend home to meet her father, the poor boy was more than a little nervous. It didn't help that Tillinghast didn't have much patience for small talk.

"Young man, there's only one thing I want to know about you," Tillinghast said.

"Yes, sir?" the man stammered.

"The results of your Wassermann test," he said.

Tillinghast was, among other things, a talented writer, and his gift with language is revealed in this description of his work at Winged Foot, where he built two of his finest courses.

"As the various holes came to life, they were of a sturdy breed. The contouring of the greens places a premium on the placement of drives, but never is there the necessity of facing a prodigious carry of the sink-or-swim sort. It is only the knowledge that the next shot must be played with rifle accuracy that brings the realization that the drive must be placed. The holes are like men, all rather similar from foot to neck, but with the greens showing the same varying character as human faces."

One of Pete Dye's earliest and best designs is the Harbour Town Golf Links on Hilton Head Island. It's been one of the most popular courses on the PGA Tour since it hosted its first tournament in 1969. Of course, Pete Dye being Pete Dye, he couldn't resist a little fine-tuning. In fact, he didn't try very hard to resist.

On one hole, there was a large, specimen pine tree protecting the left side of the green. Something about it had bothered Dye right from the start, but he couldn't quite figure out what it was. After watching play on the first day of the inaugural tournament, he realized that the tree was forcing players to drive the ball out to the right side of the fairway, taking a waste bunker out of play.

Hating decisions made by committee, Dye did the only logical thing: that night, under the cover of darkness, he sneaked out to the course with a chain saw and cut down the tree.

That Oakmont Country Club outside Pittsburgh is one of the world's most demanding courses shouldn't come as a surprise to anyone familiar with William Fownes, who, along with his father, Henry, were the guiding forces behind the design and development of the course. His philosophy was simple and to the point:

"A shot that is poorly played should be a stroke irrevocably lost."

And nowhere is that truer than at Oakmont. Take, for example, the case of Charlie Sifford in the second round of the 1973 U.S. Open. Playing the 431-yard, par-4 7th hole, Sifford hit a good drive and reached the green in regulation—only to six-putt.

To say that W. C. Fownes was strong-willed is a woeful understatement. He succeeded his father as club president in 1935 and everything went along swimmingly—so to speak—until 1940, when the membership split over a proposal to build a swimming pool. Oakmont had been losing members to clubs with pools, and a faction demanded that it was time for Oakmont to keep up with the times.

Fownes headed a group that was determined that, as a golf club, Oakmont should never have a pool. In fact, they regarded even the mere suggestion as heresy. Finally, it came down to a vote and Fownes's faction lost. Fownes resigned the presidency in protest and then, for good measure, quit the club, too.

TOMMY ARMOUR

Following a brilliant playing career that saw him win a British Open, a U.S. Open, and a PGA Championship—just for highlights—Tommy Armour became a celebrated teaching professional, most notably at Winged Foot Golf Club, outside New York City. Armour could be gruff and imperious, but he had a keen eye for both talent and the golf swing. Beginners and pros alike sought out his advice and opinions.

One day a promising young player on the PGA Tour visited Winged Foot, and Armour went out to check out the man's game. After watching the player spray one drive after another, Armour had seen enough and went back to the clubhouse.

"What do you think, Tommy?" he was asked. "He's got a beautiful swing, doesn't he?"

"Oh yes, it's beautiful," Armour replied. "The problem is, it doesn't work."

Armour was one of the first celebrity teaching professionals and, as such, charged the princely sum of $100

an hour for his lessons. And this was in the '50s and '60s, when $100 was really $100. Of course, it didn't hurt that he was giving lessons to swells who could easily afford it.

Ken Venturi, the 1964 U.S. Open champion and a highly respected teacher in his own right, was once asked why Armour charged so much for his lessons. Venturi thought for a moment.

"Maybe he didn't want to give a lot of lessons," Venturi replied, logically.

AUGUSTA NATIONAL GOLF CLUB

The Masters has always been televised under a series of one-year contracts with CBS Sports. Since it is one of the premier events in sports, this arrangement gives Augusta National tremendous leverage when it comes not only to negotiating the terms of the agreements but also to influencing the quality of the telecasts. Nobody understood this better than Clifford Roberts, who cofounded the club with Bobby Jones.

Once a year Roberts would travel to New York to meet with CBS executives, who went out of their way to make sure everything humanly possible was done to keep Mr. Roberts happy—right down to the snacks that were served. They never varied from year to year.

Tea and Oreo cookies—with the vanilla cream icing removed.

Roberts was a brilliant investor who made millions in the stock market. Because he was very fond of Byron Nelson, he offered to help Nelson with his investments. When Nelson told him of his plans to eventually retire from golf and buy a ranch in Texas, Roberts was skeptical. Still, Nelson was determined, and in 1946 he virtually retired from competitive golf.

Several years later, he got a phone call from Roberts.

"Byron, somebody just told me that Ben Hogan and some partners are building a golf course a few miles from your ranch," Roberts said. "Is that correct?"

Byron said that it was.

"They tell me that Ben and his people bought twenty-five hundred acres and they paid $3,500 an acre," Roberts said.

"I believe that's right," Byron said.

"Didn't you once tell me that you paid just $82 an acre for your ranch?" Roberts asked.

"That's right," Byron said.

"Byron, the next time we sit down to discuss your investments, remind me to treat you with more respect," Roberts said.

It's unlikely there is anyplace in America where golf's history and traditions are more deeply revered than they are at Augusta National. Just ask Nick Price.

In 1986, Price came to the 18th green on Saturday needing to make a thirty-foot putt for a course-record 62. Price, who had made ten birdies in his round, hit a great putt. It looked in all the way, but at the last second it rimmed out.

"It was eerie," said Price. "It was as if the hand of Bobby Jones reached down and flicked the ball away. It was like he was saying, 'Now, Nick, 63 is enough.'"

Incidentally, even though he had retired from competitive golf in 1930, Jones shot a 64 in a practice round prior to the 1936 Masters.

World War II caused the cancellation of the Masters from 1943 until 1946. In those years, cattle grazed on the course and the maintenance, such as it was, was provided by a most unlikely source: forty-two German prisoners of war from nearby Fort Gordon.

"It's time to go back to running a tournament," Clifford Roberts said when he announced that the Masters would resume. "We're tired of being farmers and raising chickens and goats."

Here's a good trivia question: Who was the first player to win a Green Jacket? If your answer is Horton Smith, who won the first Masters in 1934, you're wrong. The first year the winner received a Green Jacket was 1949, and it went to Sam Snead for the first of three Masters victories.

An invitation to attend the Masters is every golfer's dream. Couple that with a chance to play the course and stay at the club and you've got an opportunity that's almost impossible to pass up—as a man found out a couple years ago.

"A friend of mine got a call from one of his clients inviting him to come to Augusta, play the course, and stay for the tournament," remembers Eric Reimer, a Los Angeles lawyer and a former member of the USC golf team. "The only problem was that it conflicted with his daughter's wedding. He asked her if she could change the dates.

"'Look at it this way,' the man said to his daughter. 'The odds of you getting married are much better than the odds of me getting an invitation like this.'"

Did it work?

"Are you kidding?" Reimer says with a laugh. "But he thought it was worth a try."

The Masters is known as the "toughest ticket in sports," and with good reason. The club stopped taking names for the waiting list several years ago. Scalpers can make a fortune selling tickets. People resort to all sorts of schemes to get their hands on a badge.

A few years ago, a man was whiling away an evening at one of the many bars that dot Washington Road near Augusta National. As the night wore on, he struck up a conversation with a woman and, naturally, one thing led to another. Soon they were back at his hotel room.

After a few minutes, he excused himself and went into the bathroom. When he came out, the woman was gone. In a panic, he quickly searched his room.

His wallet was there and no money had been taken.

His car keys were still on the dresser, and so was his gold Rolex watch.

He assumed the woman had simply gotten cold feet and left. For a moment he began to relax. Then he realized what was missing.

His clubhouse badge for the Masters.

The Masters wasn't always so popular. In the first year, the members had to pass a hat to cover the purse. For many years the tickets were priced at $3, which Clifford Roberts felt wasn't enough. He wanted to raise the price to $5, but other members of the tournament committee were afraid that might be too steep an increase. To no one's surprise, the prices were raised.

On the first day of the tournament, Roberts and another committee member stood on the clubhouse porch and watched the galleries jam their way down Magnolia Lane.

"Five dollars, five dollars, five dollars," Roberts said as the people walked past.

People collect all kinds of memorabilia from the Masters. They leave the course loaded down with shirts, sweaters, photographs, and all sorts of other wonderful stuff. In 1997, Masters rookie Paul Stankowski was no different. Well, actually he was a little bit more creative than most.

After missing the cut, he took a cup with a Masters logo on the side, went out to the course, and filled it with sand from one of the bunkers.

"I mean, you never know if you'll be invited back, right?" he told a reporter.

THE BOYS

"The Boys" love almost everything about golf, except that it sometimes involves playing with women. It's not that they have anything against women, per se. It's just that in the best of all worlds, the golf course would simply be an extension of the men's locker room. Or better yet, the men's grill.

One day my friend Dennis Powell was asked if he'd be willing to fill a spot in a mixed tournament. He politely declined.

"There's two things I don't do," he said. "Dance with boys and play golf with girls."

If you're one of The Boys, the highlights of the golf season include the big three-day member-guest tournament and the club championships. Not so much because of the competition, but because they're perfect times to party.

One day a friend approached Dennis Powell and asked him how he stood in his match.

"I've got him right where I want him," Dennis said. "He's three up with three holes to go, and I'm out of beer."

Naturally, since these tournaments involve heavy doses of partying, this sometimes takes its toll on The Boys, no matter how tournament-tough they might be—in a manner of speaking.

"I knew it was a good party last night, but I didn't realize just how good it was until we got to the first green this morning and one of the guys marked his ball with an Advil," remembers my friend Dave Wertz.

It's not true that to be one of The Boys you have to work on Wall Street, but apparently it helps. And since Wall Street is, at its core, legalized gambling taken to the highest level, it only follows that The Boys love to have all sort of bets and side bets going on the golf course. In fact, sometimes the betting scarcely leaves room for the golf itself.

"I was playing with Dennis one day, and when we finished the front nine he let us know how all the bets stood," remembers Tim Cassidy. "There was the front nine, the presses, the sandies, greenies, Watsons, Hogans, and everything else. When he got finished, I asked him what I shot.

"'I don't know,' he said. 'There wasn't any room left on the card for the scores.'"

For The Boys, the fun and games don't end on the 18th green. Grillrooms and patios from coast to coast echo with the sound of dice landing on tables as players roll for drinks, sometimes for hours on end.

One afternoon I brought my son, Ben, then in second grade, to the course for some quality time together. We stopped by the patio to visit friends, and Ben became fascinated by the dice games.

The next day at school, his teacher asked the class if anyone had done anything over the weekend that they wished to share during show-and-tell. Ben raised his hand.

"Mr. Vanneck taught me how to roll for drinks," he said proudly.

For The Boys, the ideal club would have a course, a men's grill, a locker room, and not much else. A couple of tennis courts, perhaps, but definitely not a pool.

"I went to the pool once, but I hated it," Dennis Powell told a friend. "It reminded me of Vietnam—hot, noisy, and crowded. I never went back."

In recent years, the growing popularity of golf and the maturing of the baby-boom generation have led to longer and longer waiting lists at country clubs, particularly in the larger metropolitan areas.

Increasingly, many clubs have begun admitting "limited golf" members, who can play only at certain days and hours of the week. Eventually, as older members either leave a club or give up their golf privileges, people move up the waiting list to full golf status. Naturally, some people are more patient than others.

One of The Boys was on the waiting list for a full golf membership at a club in one of New York City's wealthiest suburbs. As he drove past the club on his way back from the train station early one summer evening, he noticed that the American flag was flying at half-mast. He turned into the parking lot and walked into the clubhouse. At the front desk he asked the receptionist the first question that had popped into his mind:

"Was he a golf member?"

THE BRITISH OPEN

The British Open is one of the truly great events in sports; it is televised around the world and attracts enormous galleries. Many people consider it the true world championship of golf, given the international field it traditionally attracts. Like so much of golf, it wasn't always this way. As late as the 1960s, it had more than its share of quirks.

In 1962, Jack Nicklaus was the reigning U.S. Open and U.S. Amateur champion. Naturally, you would expect that the R & A would treat him as one of the game's premier players when he arrived at Troon.

Not exactly.

They gave him a 3:45 starting time in the first round. And to add insult to injury, they paired him with a marker.

When it was brought to the R & A's attention that this might be considered poor form bordering on an insult, they moved to correct the situation. More or less.

They put Nicklaus out with two other players. At the very back of the field.

JACK BURKE JR.

There's always been a certain irrefutable logic to the thinking of Jackie Burke, the winner of both the 1956 Masters and the 1956 PGA Championship.

On the verge of the 1997 season, Steve Elkington—a friend and admirer—told Burke that his clubs had been stolen.

"So what?" Burke said. "You weren't winning with them anyway. Good riddance."

Sure enough, Elkington got a new set and won in both Los Angeles and at The Players Championship.

CADDIES

The final day of the Ryder Cup matches is always tense and exciting, but that was particularly true in 1995 at Oak Hill, when the Americans watched their lead disappear in the singles competition.

As one match came to the tee on the par-3 15th hole, the caddie for an American player searched for the yardage plate set into the ground. He finally located it, under the foot of a man wearing the blue European team jacket.

"Get the hell off that marker," the caddie said, glaring at the man, who immediately apologized.

After the players hit their tee shots, a man walked up to the caddie as he prepared to leave the tee.

"See here, young man," he said. "You can't talk to Prince Andrew that way."

Like everything else these days, people routinely bet on golf events, particularly big ones like the Ryder Cup. As you might expect, caddies are not immune to the temptation. Of course, sometimes betting is costly. And some bets are more costly than others. Take the case of one Dan Stojak.

Stojak was Loren Roberts's caddie in the 1995 Ryder Cup. He put $1,000 down with a bookie in Las Vegas—on the European team. When they won, he made a handsome profit.

He also was fired when Roberts heard about the bet.

"I've met a number of inspirational people in my life, but I've always been taken by the example of a young man who caddied for me in the Miami Open," two-time PGA champion Paul Runyan once told a writer. "He'd had polio and his legs were badly damaged. When I saw him limp over I began taking clubs out of my bag, and this insulted him terribly. He told me to put them back, that he didn't want pity and he just wanted a chance to prove he could do anything the other caddies could do. I was skeptical but agreed to give him a try. He turned out to be a wonderful caddie, and we stayed in touch for many years. In fact, when he graduated from high school I was delighted to help him get a job."

Dow Finsterwald, the 1958 PGA champion, was one of the favorites going into the 1960 U.S. Open at Cherry Hills. Playing the 16th hole in his first round, he asked his caddie what club he should hit for his second shot.

"Why should I bother?" the caddie said. "You haven't taken my advice yet."

Finsterwald glared at the caddie and then pulled a club from his bag.

"That's not enough," the caddie said.

Finsterwald used the club anyway, and he wasn't any too pleased when his ball came up short of the green.

The caddie never saw the 17th hole. Finsterwald fired him on the spot.

Much has been written about Ben Crenshaw's emotional victory in the 1995 Masters, coming as it did just after the death of his longtime teacher and friend, Harvey Penick. The emotion of that victory is vividly captured in the photos of Crenshaw collapsing in tears and being consoled by his caddie, Carl Jackson, after holing out on the last green. As it turned out, Jackson's role in Ben's win went far beyond merely carrying his bag.

Ben Crenshaw is, at heart, a fervent traditionalist. So it is no surprise that when Augusta National changed its rule requiring players to use the club's caddies, Crenshaw stayed with Jackson, a local caddie who had packed his bag since 1976.

Crenshaw had come to Augusta struggling with his swing and with little real hope of duplicating his 1984 victory. But Jackson, after spending some time with Crenshaw on the practice tee, gave his friend some advice.

"Look, you've got to get that ball back a little bit in your stance and then just tighten up your backswing," he said. "Just keep your left arm right there close to your body and turn those shoulders like you used to."

Almost immediately, the crispness returned to Crenshaw's

ball-striking and he felt his confidence return—so much so that he told his brother that he truly believed this might be his week. Something he rarely, if ever, did.

When Cecil Timms learned that he would be caddying for Ben Hogan in the 1953 British Open at Carnoustie, he told friends he felt honored, if a little intimidated.

When the tournament ended and Hogan had won, Timms felt something else: lucky.

Hogan paid him £300—the exact amount he won and an altogether princely sum for a caddie in postwar Scotland.

If you're a caddie, this is your worst nightmare come true. You're in the last round of a tournament and your player has the lead and a good chance to pick up his first win as a pro. He's looking at a birdie putt and asks you to tend the pin. He strokes the putt, and as it starts rolling toward the hole you try to pull out the flagstick.

It's stuck, so you try to loosen it. No luck—the ball is getting closer and closer. So, in desperation, you yank on the pin and pull the cup out of the ground, just in time for the ball to bounce off it and carom away. You realize that you have single-handedly—so to speak—turned a birdie into a double bogey and cost your player the win.

To make matters worse, your player is Jack Nicklaus.

Years ago, the caddies at Seminole were known to gamble a little bit on the outcome of the matches their players were involved in. One such match involved President John F. Kennedy.

Kennedy was taking his time reading a putt. Customarily, people are pretty generous when it comes to giving putts to presidents, but this was a delicate little putt at a crucial point in the match. As Kennedy approached his ball one of his opponents said, "That's good. Pick it up, Mr. President."

"No," one of the caddies inadvertently called out.

Kennedy looked over at him and started laughing.

An American traveled to Scotland to try to qualify for the 1927 British Open at St. Andrews. When he reached the course, he was assigned a weathered, wizened old caddie who, despite the relatively warm weather, was wearing an old Chesterfield coat he claimed had been given to him by former British prime minister David Lloyd-George.

After a few holes, the American began to worry about the caddie's health and asked him if he was going to be able to finish his round.

"I'll be fine, sir," the caddie said. "I'm afraid I had a wee bit too much of the drink last night. It's funny how the drink creeps up on you sometimes. By the time I got home I was so drunk me own dog bit me."

Mike Mazzeo caddied for Fuzzy Zoeller for almost twenty years, and you would expect that after all that time he'd be able to read his man's moods. Apparently not.

Mazzeo showed up late one day during the 1995 Tournament Players Championship and told Zoeller he was "on a work slowdown because I haven't been making much money lately."

"You're making less now," Zoeller said just before he fired him.

AL CAPONE

One day Al Capone, weary from overseeing his criminal empire, decided to take the afternoon off for a little golf. And who can blame him? Bootlegging, prostitution, numbers running, loan-sharking, murder, and all the other nefarious activities of a crime boss would wear out even the strongest of men.

Alas, poor Al couldn't quite manage to leave his work at the office. It seems that his caddie dropped Capone's bag near a green, setting off a pistol stashed inside and wounding Capone slightly. It's not clear whether Capone finished his round. It's also not clear what happened to his caddie—although it's a safe bet he didn't bring home much of a tip.

BING CROSBY

Bing Crosby was an excellent golfer, talented enough to play in both the U.S. and British Amateurs.

Late one afternoon he was minding his own business, hitting practice balls off the 10th tee at Bel-Air Country Club in Los Angeles. A particularly officious member of the greens committee spotted him and ordered him to stop. He did. Then, without saying a word, he went in, cleaned out his locker, and resigned from the club on the spot.

JOHN DALY

Peter Thomson, the great Australian who won five British Opens, traveled to St. Andrews for the 1993 Dunhill Cup, an international team competition.

One afternoon, Thomson sat in his corner room in the Old Course Hotel with a writer from the United States. As they talked, with Thomson's beloved classical music playing softly in the background, they watched groups play into the 16th green and then hit their tee shots on 17, a difficult par 4. Eventually John Daly's group came into view, and the writer asked Thomson for his thoughts on the man who had won the 1991 PGA Championship with an audacious display of power and touch.

"I fancy that he has as much natural ability as either Sam Snead or Seve Ballesteros, and that is high praise indeed," Thomson said. "But there is a certain sadness to him. I don't think he really likes himself, and you can see that he's not happy. I don't reckon you can play this game to your fullest capacity unless you're happy with yourself. I think he'll win tournaments, but will he ever become the supreme champion that his talent would suggest? I'm afraid the answer is probably no."

If John Daly has known his share of ups and downs with his golf career, they pale in comparison to the turmoil in his personal life. At age thirty-one, he's already facing his third divorce. At least he's able to joke about it, though.

In the 1994 Masters, he was paired with Ian Woosnam for all four rounds. After he came off the course on Sunday, he joked to reporters that "maybe Woosie and I should get married. It's the longest good relationship I've ever had."

JIMMY DEMARET

Jimmy Demaret was a close friend of Don Cherry, the popular singer who was also a talented golfer. This makes a certain amount of sense, since Demaret was a popular golfer who was also a talented singer.

The friendship, however, didn't stop Demaret from playing practical jokes on Cherry. One of his favorites was to slip into the back of the room during one of Cherry's performances and, in the middle of a particularly romantic ballad, bounce a handful of golf balls along the floor.

Jimmy Demaret was walking through a clubhouse following a round when he watched a small boy approach a prominent player and ask for his autograph. The player refused, and the boy was crestfallen.

"Come here, son," Demaret said to the boy. "I may have forgotten how to play, but I still know how to write."

A young man approached Jimmy Demaret and wondered if he could get some advice.

"Mr. Demaret, I drive the ball long and straight," he said nervously. "I'm a good iron player. I'm especially good with my 1-iron. All my friends say I'm a good putter. What should I do?"

Demaret looked at him, took a sip of his drink, and pondered the question for what seemed to the young man to be an eternity.

"Join the Tour before you find out how hard the game really is," Demaret joked.

For a time, Jimmy Demaret endorsed a steel-centered ball made by First Flight. Their advertising featured Demaret claiming that the ball went farther and straighter and so on and so forth.

One year he was playing well and in contention at the Masters until he hit balls into the water on both the 12th and 15th holes. When he walked into the locker room he ran into Sam Snead, who couldn't resist giving him the needle.

"Jimmy, those old 'steelies' may be as good as you claim, but they can't float," he said.

DISASTERS

There are more than a few "what-ifs" in Phil Rodgers's career. The 1958 NCAA champion won five times on the PGA Tour, but lost the 1963 British Open in a thirty-six-hole playoff to New Zealand's Bob Charles. The year before, he came within two strokes of joining Jack Nicklaus and Arnold Palmer in their historic playoff in the U.S. Open at Oakmont. That he even got that close is remarkable.

In the first round he came to the 315-yard, par-4 17th hole and decided to try to drive the green. Sadly, his ball came to rest in the branches of a newly planted evergreen that guarded the corner of the dogleg.

Rodgers carefully studied the situation and decided to try to play the ball. Instead of escaping from the tree, his ball simply fell to a lower branch. He tried again, with the same result. Finally, on his third try, the ball fell to earth, but by the time he was finished he had taken a quadruple-bogey 8 and had seemingly shot himself out of the Open.

To his considerable credit, though, Rodgers scrambled back and at one point briefly held the lead in the final round before coming up just short. Still, it was a remarkable comeback.

There is really no way of knowing if this story is true, but even if it's only remotely accurate, it records the ultimate exercise in futility. According to legend, a man named A. J. Lewis was playing a course in Sussex, England, and on one green he took over a hundred putts before picking up. He never did hole out. Even more tragic—or at least unbelievable—is the sad story of Andrew Kirkaldy, who, in contention to win the 1889 British Open, missed a one-inch putt. It so unnerved him that he fell completely apart, finally finishing second to Willie Park Jr.

Women's professional golf in Europe is a dicey proposition at best. The purses are small. The courses aren't all that great. The administration of play can sometimes be haphazard. Then there are the caddies—when you can find one.

A woman named Kristel Mourgue d'Algue was playing in the Marks & Spencer Open, and instead of pulling a cart as she usually did, she decided to splurge and take a caddie.

On a par-3 hole, Ms. Mourgue d'Algue hit it within inches of the hole. To her great horror, she watched as her caddie put the club back in the bag of one of her playing partners. Since they were both playing the same clubs, it was a mistake anyone could make. Well, maybe not just anyone. Maybe just someone who'd never caddied before. At any rate, on the heels of her two-stroke penalty, she fired her hapless caddie before any more damage could be done.

Some of the best and most strategic holes in golf are short par 4s, and one of the best of this breed is the 324-yard 6th hole on Winged Foot's West Course. How tough is it? Consider the plight of Bill Mehlhorn in the 1929 U.S. Open.

Mehlhorn hit a fine drive, and with a short iron in his hand for his second shot, he decided to shoot at a pin tucked close behind a bunker guarding the right side of the green. He cut it too close and wound up putting the ball in the bunker. Then his troubles really began.

Mehlhorn bladed his third shot, sending it screaming over the green and down a slope into a creek. Several of his next few shots caromed off trees, and by the time he was through he had a 10 on his scorecard and had seen all he wanted to see of Winged Foot.

BOB DRUM

The late Bob Drum and Arnold Palmer had a long friendship that dated back to the days when "the Drummer"
covered the teenage Palmer as a writer for the *Pittsburgh
Post*. According to Drum, he was the man who invented the
modern "Grand Slam"; it happened during a conversation
with Palmer after the 1960 U.S. Open at Cherry Hills.

"I wanted to go to the British Open, but I knew the morons
I worked for would never send me," Drum once recalled.
"They didn't have a clue what the British Open was all about,
so I had to think of a way to make it seem like the biggest
deal in the world. Anyway, Arnold and I are on this plane and
we were talking about Bobby Jones. I asked him if he thought
anyone would ever do what Jones did, winning the 'Grand
Slam'—both the U.S. and British Opens and Amateurs.
Arnold said there was no way. So I said what about winning
the Masters, the U.S. Open, the British Open, and the PGA
Championship? Since he'd already won the Masters and the
Open, it started him thinking. I said, 'You're already halfway
there. If you won the British Open and the PGA you'd win
the "Grand Slam," too.'

"Well, Arnold said he thought he could do it and I started
writing about how he was going to try and win the 'Grand
Slam,'" the Drummer went on. "The other writers picked up

38

on it, and it became such a big story that they had to send me over."

Palmer went on to finish second at the British Open. He never did manage to win the PGA Championship.

FOREIGN AFFAIRS

One of the charms of international events such as the World Cup or the World Amateur Team Championship is that they draw players from small countries that don't have a chance in the world of winning—indeed, many don't have a chance of breaking 80—but come for the sheer sportsmanship of it all. Take the case of Switzerland's Hans Schweizer, who played in the 1960 World Amateur Team Championship at Merion.

Teeing off on the first day, he was visibly nervous. After his round, writers asked him if it was disconcerting to play in front of a crowd.

"Oh, yes," he said. "Before today only cows had seen me play."

WALTER HAGEN

Hagen began his professional career as an assistant pro at the Country Club of Rochester. The professional was a transplanted Scotsman named Andrew Christy, who helped Hagen develop his game to the point where Hagen soon became confident he could beat him.

Bad idea.

One day Hagen strode into the pro shop and issued his boss a challenge.

"C'mon, Mr. Christy," Hagen said. "Let's go out and see if you can beat me."

There was dead silence in the shop. Christy glared at Hagen, his face turning red with anger. The other people in the shop carefully studied their shoes. It was several moments before he spoke.

"Sonny, when I want to play golf with you I'll do the asking, not you," he said, then turned and walked out of the shop.

To say that Walter Hagen had an eye for women is a colossal understatement.

Playing in the 1914 U.S. Open at Midlothian Country Club, he opened with rounds of 68-74-73 and was cruising along to what appeared to be certain victory—until late in the final round. The problem was that, standing on the 15th tee, he decided to strike up a conversation with a beautiful, brown-haired, green-eyed nineteen-year-old he had spotted in his gallery.

"Do you play golf?" Hagen asked.

"No," she said. "But I'd like to."

"Would you like me to give you a lesson?" Hagen asked.

"Oh, yes," she said. "I'd like that very much."

"Fine, I'll meet you tonight at eight," Hagen said, then returned to his golf.

Now utterly distracted, Hagen proceeded to three-putt both 16 and 17 before getting his mind back on golf. He finished with a total of 292, edging the great amateur Chick Evans.

After the awards ceremony, Hagen's friends went looking for him so the real celebration could begin. No chance. Hagen was off to find his date.

No one could ever say Walter Hagen didn't have his priorities in order.

In 1942, during the darkest days of World War II, golf impresario Fred Corcoran learned that he had to travel to London on business. His friend, Walter Hagen, told him to go to the Savoy Hotel and introduce himself to the hotel manager, Karl Hefflin.

Corcoran arrived at the hotel, went to the front desk, and asked to speak with Mr. Hefflin, telling the clerk that he was Hagen's friend. A few minutes later, Hefflin arrived, looking very grim. When he saw Corcoran, a look of relief swept over his face.

"The boy misunderstood," Hefflin explained. "He said Walter Hagen was here. We'd been bombed by the Nazis three times in the past month. I was just wondering how I was supposed to cope with the blitz and Walter Hagen, too."

Walter Hagen was a keen student of human nature, which is one reason he was so devastatingly effective in match-play competitions such as the PGA Championship and the Ryder Cup.

Hagen was the captain of the American team that traveled to Southport and Ainsdale for the 1937 Ryder Cup matches. It would mark his last appearance as a member of a Ryder Cup team, and the first of nine appearances for Sam Snead. The British public had heard a great deal about Snead, and anticipation ran high as the first day's matches approached. Naturally, when Hagen decided to hold Snead out of the four-somes competition, it created a huge controversy. Hagen later explained his decision.

"Sam's just a kid," he told a friend. "He's never even seen a foursomes match, let alone played in one. It's a different kind of pressure. If he got shellacked it could break his spirit, and I'd hate to see that happen."

There was more than a touch of the showman in Walter Hagen, and he used this to particularly good effect in match-play situations.

In one tournament, he came to the final hole with the match all square. He pushed his drive into the rough, with a stand of trees between his ball and the green. His opponent's drive landed in the heart of the fairway.

Things clearly looked bad for Hagen. He paced around, dramatically studying all his options. Finally, he pulled a lofted club from his bag and motioned the gallery away, indicating that his only play was to pitch the ball back to the fairway. He addressed and was about to hit his shot, when he suddenly backed away and looked at the trees blocking his path to the green. As the crowd roared its approval, he put the club back in the bag, took another, and played a beautiful punch shot through the trees and onto the green. Flustered, his opponent played a poor second shot and lost the hole. Later, a friend praised Hagen for playing such a brave shot.

"Brave?" Hagen said. "Christ, I could have driven a truck through those trees."

Practice, as we know it today, was almost unheard of in Walter Hagen's day. For that reason, or perhaps because he was an uncommonly gifted athlete in the first place, he never understood why players would stand on a practice tee hitting balls hour after hour.

"I don't get it," he said to a friend one day as they stood by a practice tee during a tournament. "These guys already know how to hit the ball. It's a waste of time. I'd be afraid to practice like that. I might find out a way to do something wrong. These guys aren't getting any better. They're just punishing themselves."

CLAUDE HARMON

Claude Harmon won the 1948 Masters and was the long-time professional at both Winged Foot and Seminole. It's not surprising, then, that his four sons became not only fine players but respected teaching professionals in their own right as well. While he worked with his sons on developing sound swings, he never lost sight of what was really important in golf—scoring.

"Claude used a trick with the boys that he sometimes used with guys who were his assistants," Dave Marr once recalled. "If he thought you were getting too mechanical, he'd take half the clubs out of your bag and then send you out to play. It forced you to hit shots and think about getting the ball into the hole. It was a great lesson."

BEN HOGAN

In a rare—and celebrated—interview with CBS Sports, Ben Hogan told Ken Venturi that he was glad he wasn't born into wealth, because he enjoyed knowing that he had worked for everything he'd accomplished. If that's the case, he has much to be glad about.

Hogan's father committed suicide when Ben was just six. Some reports indicate that he might have been in the room when his father shot himself. Young Ben would tag along with his older brother, Royal, as he sold newspapers to help support the family. Soon, Ben was selling papers as well. But on the eve of his twelfth birthday, he began caddying at Glen Garden Country Club—a seven-mile walk from his home. The pay was a princely 65 cents a bag, with a dime tip for an exceptional job. If a kid was lucky—and got to the course early—he might get out twice a day.

Young Ben might not have known much about luck, but he did know about getting to the course early. Many nights, if it wasn't too cold or too rainy, he would sleep in one of the bunkers and rise with the sun to be first in line.

Hogan's intensity extended well beyond the golf course. In fact, it extended beyond his waking hours.

"Ben and I traveled together a little bit when we first came on tour," Byron Nelson remembers. "One night I heard this noise and I thought there were rats in the room. I turned on the lights to see where the noise was coming from. It was Ben grinding his teeth in his sleep. I told Jimmy Demaret about it. He said not to worry, it was just Ben 'sharpening those old Blue Blades [a popular brand of razor blades] of his.'"

Hogan was also legendary for his ability to concentrate during a round.

In the 1948 U.S. Open, he was paired with George Fazio in the second round. Fazio holed his second shot for an eagle on one hole, but when the time came to sign his scorecard, Hogan said he didn't remember the shot and wanted to wait for confirmation. Fazio, a friend of Hogan's, was incredulous and thought Hogan was kidding.

He wasn't. He literally could not remember seeing the shot.

As Ben Hogan aged into his seventies and eighties, old friends would occasionally meet him for lunch at his club, Shady Oaks. The visits no doubt meant as much to

Hogan as they did to his friends. One afternoon Dave Marr was in Fort Worth and met Hogan for lunch.

"We had a wonderful time, talking about old times and mutual friends," Marr remembered. "At the end of the lunch, Ben sat there, very quietly, carefully shining the silverware with his napkin. Finally, he looked up at me with tears in his eyes and said, 'Dave, do you know what I really miss? God, I miss tournament golf.'

"It made the hair stand up on the back of my neck."

One of the most famous photographs in sports is Hy Peskin's classic shot of Hogan hitting his approach to the 18th hole in the final round of the 1950 U.S. Open at Merion. Galleries lined the fairways and surrounded the green, looking on as Hogan rifled a 1-iron from just over 200 yards. The ball ended up some forty feet from the hole. Hogan got down in two and the next day beat George Fazio and Lloyd Mangrum in a playoff. It was his first win in a Major championship following his near-fatal automobile accident.

Later, a writer asked Hogan how he was able to pull off such a difficult shot under such incredible pressure.

"I've been practicing that shot since I was twelve years old," Hogan said.

Ben Hogan turned pro when he was seventeen, but his debut was anything but auspicious. In his first tournament he shot an opening-round 78, followed it with a 75, and promptly withdrew.

Years later, a writer asked Hogan what he'd learned from that early failure. If he was expecting a deep, cosmic answer, he was disappointed.

"I learned I had no business being there," Hogan said.

It would be eight long years before Hogan would get his first win—years that would see him go broke and leave the Tour three times.

Don January grew up in Texas and, naturally, was a great admirer of Ben Hogan. And since he was one of the state's finest amateurs, Hogan was familiar with January as well.

January joined the PGA Tour in 1956 and promptly won the Dallas Centennial Open, establishing himself as one of the top young players. One day in his rookie year he happened to be practicing next to Ben Hogan. Summoning what must have been considerable nerve, he asked what Hogan thought of his swing.

There was silence as Hogan—as was his nature—carefully considered his answer.

"Something wrong with your elbow?" Hogan finally answered, then turned and walked away.

Armed—so to speak—with this revelation, January set out to correct the position of his left arm at address. He practiced and practiced and practiced. He read Hogan's books and instruction articles in the magazines. Then he practiced some more.

It wasn't until years later that he finally figured it out.

Hogan was talking about his right elbow.

Bill Collins was another fine player who sought out Hogan for advice. They were playing a practice round together and had a $20 bet on the line. Finally, late in the round, Collins asked Hogan for advice.

"What do you think I should work on, Ben?" he asked.

Hogan looked at him and then took a long drag on his cigarette.

"How's the match stand?" Hogan asked.

"You could play a whole round with Ben and he might not say ten words to you," Tommy Bolt remembers. "But if you hit a great shot—not a lucky shot but a great shot—he'd say 'Good shot' and really mean it. Man, that was like getting a three-page letter from anyone else."

In his later years, Hogan enjoyed eating lunch at his club in Fort Worth, Shady Oaks. A table was always reserved for him with a view overlooking the golf course. Occasionally, he would offer advice to his fellow members.

One day he ran into a friend in the locker room. Hogan asked the man how he was playing.

"Just awful," the man said. "I can't seem to figure out what's wrong. I'm so frustrated."

"I know," Hogan said. "I've been watching you, and it's painful. If you don't mind, I could give you a tip."

Naturally, the man was delighted, and for a good half hour Hogan broke down the man's swing and told him what corrections he had to make. Later, another friend asked the man if the advice had worked.

"Yes and no," the man said. "He cured my slice. The problem is, it took me a month to get rid of my new hook."

Ben Hogan shot rounds of 70-69-66-69—274—to win the 1953 Masters, the first of the three Major championships he would win that year. His 14-under-par total easily beat Porky Oliver, whose total of 279 tied the previous Masters record and would have won any of the previous sixteen tournaments.

"That's as good as I can play," Hogan said after the tournament. "I'd just like to come back and play as well next year."

"If you do, Ben, you'll be out here by yourself," said his old friend and rival, Byron Nelson. "No one else will bother to show up."

In 1965, Ben Hogan and Sam Snead played a match for the old "Shell's Wonderful World of Golf" series. The match was played at Houston Country Club, and it was a classic. Hogan hit every fairway and every green, and shot a 3-under-par 69. His approach shots were astonishingly accurate, leaving him one birdie putt after another. Gene Sarazen, the commentator for the match, called it the finest round of golf he'd ever seen.

For his part, Sam played pretty well, until he fell behind late in the match and began pressing. He wound up shooting an even-par 72.

In the postmatch interview, Hogan thanked Snead for the match and said he enjoyed it. Then he added, "You know, Sam, if you'd have hit it a little closer, we'd have had a little closer match."

Nobody could ever argue with Ben Hogan's logic.

After the match, an elderly member approached Hogan and congratulated him on his fine play. But he couldn't resist giving Hogan a bit of advice.

"You know, Ben, on that putt you missed on 13, your stance was way too open," the man said.

Beautiful.

People who saw Hogan in his prime say that when he hit the ball it sounded different from everyone else's shots. They use terms like "crisper" and "sharper."

One day Jay Hebert and Jimmy Demaret were in the locker room changing into their spikes. Through an open window Herbert could hear balls being struck on the nearby practice tee.

"They all sounded pretty much the same," Hebert recalled. "But every thirty seconds or so there'd be a *pow*. I looked at Jimmy and he said, 'Ben's out there early today.'"

"Everyone talks about how Ben loved to practice, and that was true," Dave Marr once remembered. "But he loved to experiment. He'd hit all kinds of weird shots in practice rounds, just in case a situation came up in a tournament that might demand just that shot. One year we were playing a practice round at Augusta. We both hit good drives and good second shots on the [par-5] 13th. I started walking toward the hole, and Ben stopped and dropped another ball. Now he's got this ugly downhill lie to a green fronted by water. He took his 4-wood, choked down, and hit a low hook. The ball barely cleared the water, but instead of coming in hot like you might expect, it landed softly and rolled to a stop about fifteen feet from the flag. I heard him call me.

"'David,' he said. 'That might be the best shot you'll ever see.'"

When he played his practice rounds prior to a tournament, Hogan rarely shot at the pins, preferring instead to hit his approach shots where he thought the pins might be set during competition. Naturally, this led to some speculation among the writers who followed Hogan during those rounds.

"They'd ask Ben why his shots were landing sixty feet from the hole," remembers Lanny Wadkins. "He'd say, 'I don't know, boys. I'm not hitting it very good. I just hope I can find out what the problem is before the tournament starts.' It was amazing how many guys never caught on."

Take a look at some of the courses where Ben Hogan won his Major championships—places like Augusta National, Merion, Carnoustie, Oakland Hills, Oakmont, and Riviera—and it becomes clear that like all great players, the tougher the course the better he liked it. One day he was playing in a tournament. As he prepared to tee off on the first hole, he looked at a leader board and saw that two players he'd barely heard of were leading with impossibly low scores.

"What am I doing playing a tournament on a course where two guys like this can shoot scores like that?" he asked a friend.

For many years, Ben Hogan was involved in a Dallas tournament to raise money for a charity, the Lighthouse for the Blind. He arranged for many of the other top players to compete, and generally the tournament did very well.

One year, however, the galleries were small, and when Hogan got ready to present the charity with a check, he paused for a minute.

"This isn't right," Hogan said.

He took $300 of his own money, put it in his hat, and then began to pass the hat. By the time he got the hat back, he had raised another $2,000.

"I met Ben when I was Claude Harmon's assistant at Seminole, and when I went out on tour I used to play practice rounds with Ben," Dave Marr remembered. "Jay Hebert and I used to play practice rounds with Ben and Claude at Augusta. We'd have a match and medal play nassau going, plus some other junk. Ben always wanted to bet on who hit the most fairways and greens. Playing that game with Ben was an invitation to lose money. I told him I thought we'd better just stick to golf."

There's a temptation to see Ben Hogan as some sort of superhuman, ball-striking machine who could win at will. And while he certainly was a formidable competitor, he was also as human as the next guy—on occasion.

The 18th hole at San Francisco's Olympic Club is a short but tight par 4. Just the kind of hole you'd figure a player like

Ben Hogan should own. But in the playoff with Jack Fleck for the 1955 U.S. Open, Hogan proved just how human he could be.

Fleck held a one-shot lead, and Hogan realized he needed to make a birdie. He hooked his tee shot badly, up onto the steep heavily roughed hillside that runs along the left side of the hole. He struggled to get the ball back to the fairway and wound up making a difficult putt for a double-bogey 6.

Hogan indicated that his right foot had slipped on the downswing. Tommy Armour wasn't buying it.

"Hogan's human after all," Armour said. "His heart slipped, that's what slipped."

In 1953, after winning the U.S. and British Opens and the Masters, Ben Hogan started a golf equipment company in his hometown, Fort Worth. A year later, dissatisfied with the first line of clubs the company manufactured, he ordered their destruction. This led to a falling-out with one of his investors, Pollard Simon. Hogan, unwilling to compromise, took out a $450,000 loan and bought Simon out.

Fort Worth is a union town, and shortly after the company got up and running, a union came in and tried to organize Hogan's workers. Hogan would hear none of it. He went to the factory and gave the assembled workers a stern rebuke.

"You clearly believe that by organizing you're going to make a lot more money and, in effect, tell me, the boss, what you're going to do," he said. "Well, before you vote, let me remind you of one thing: I've already started over once, and I can, and will, do it again if necessary. Now, so far neither I nor any of my investors have made one red cent. When I make some money I'll see that you make some, too. Until that happens, you're not going to make one penny more than I can afford to pay you."

In 1960, Hogan sold the company to American Machine and Foundry but remained actively involved as chairman. In 1988, the company was sold to a Japanese conglomerate, Cosmo World. To put it mildly, Hogan was less than thrilled about the sale. At a luncheon with the president of Cosmo World, Minoru Isutani, and several other executives, Hogan turned to them and gave them a decidedly undiplomatic piece of his mind:

"I don't know if you people understand what you just bought," he said. "This company is the crown jewels. I just hope you're smart enough not to [expletive] it up."

In 1992, *Golf Digest* assigned one of its editors, Guy Yocom, to do an extensive piece on Ben Hogan's so-called "secret," which he had revealed in an article for *Life* magazine in 1955. Yocom, a fine player in his own right, traveled to Fort Worth for a rare, face-to-face meeting with Hogan. The meeting went well enough until Yocom began to press Hogan about his secret.

"Everything I know is in the books and articles I've written," Hogan said. "Did you read them?"

Yocom assured Hogan that he had.

"Well, maybe you should read them again," Hogan replied coolly.

The conversation went on for a few more minutes until Hogan tired of the questioning.

"Look, I could spend ten minutes with you and I promise you that you'll never hit another hook again, unless you want to," Hogan said, leaning forward and staring at Yocom, his lower lip quivering.

"I don't have anything to do this afternoon, Mr. Hogan," Yocom replied, trying to break the tension.

The Great Man was not amused. The interview was over.

When Ken Venturi joined the Tour in 1957, he quickly caught Ben Hogan's attention and the two often played practice rounds together. Indeed, until he was injured in a car accident, many people predicted Venturi would become the game's dominant player in the post-Hogan era.

Over the years, many people have speculated on the true nature of Hogan's "secret." Some people say he changed his grip. Others say he changed his swing. Still others think it was just a matter of confidence—success breeding success. Venturi has his own theory.

"Ben just intimidated people," Venturi explains. "First of all, he'd outwork you. Then he'd outthink you. Then, when you arrived on the first tee, he'd look you dead in the eye. That was his way of letting you know that he owned you. You could be his best friend, but when they said 'play away' he wanted to beat you into the ground. And you know what? That's how you have to be if you're going to be a champion."

Gay Brewer, who won the 1967 Masters, met Ben Hogan as a 15-year-old caddie. When he came out on tour, Hogan was helpful with suggestions and advice—to a point.

One day Brewer approached Hogan and asked him for help with his game.

"Ben, I'm really fighting this hook," Brewer said. "If you could show me how you learned to hit that fade of yours, I'll never hit another hook again."

"It took me twenty years to learn that." Hogan said coolly. "You'll have to work that out for yourself."

HOLES IN ONE

Young Tom Morris won four straight British Opens from 1868 to 1871 before his tragic death in 1875 at age twenty-four. That would be enough to secure his place in golf history, but it's also important to note that he's credited with golf's first recorded hole in one.

Playing in the 1868 British Open at Prestwick, Scotland, he aced the 155-yard 8th hole, then went on to win by two strokes over Robert Andrew.

How difficult is it to make a hole in one? Mathematicians will give you varying odds, but back in the early 1940s a pro named Harry Gonder proved that it's not easy. Not at all.

Gonder, with a few witnesses, a caddie to tee up the balls, and one to retrieve them from the green, set out to make a hole in one on a 165-yard hole. He hit just over 1,800 balls. None went in. The closest was one that hit the pin and came to rest a few inches from the hole. After sixteen and a half hours, Harry Gonder had seen enough. He walked in.

Mr. and Mrs. Herman Tissies can tell you a thing or two about playing par 3s.

Mr. Tissies played in the 1950 British Open at Royal Troon, and there's no telling how well he might have done if it hadn't been for the short, par-3 8th—the "Postage Stamp" hole, where he unceremoniously made a 15.

His wife, Argea, had considerably better luck playing in the Italian Ladies Senior Open at Punta Ala. In 1978, she made a hole in one on the 2nd hole. Five years later, in the same tournament, on the same course, on the same hole, on the same date with the same club, she did it again.

Back-to-back aces are rare, but consider the odds of holing tee shots on consecutive par 4s. In 1964, a man named Noel Manley was playing at Del Valle Country Club in Saugus, California. He holed his tee shot on the 328-yard 7th hole, then followed that with an ace on the 300-yard 8th hole. Both holes played slightly downhill and downwind. It hardly matters.

The record for the longest hole in one belongs to one Bob Mitera, who in 1965 aced a hole with a drive of 459 yards. It, too, was downhill and downwind. And it was made on a course named—of all things—Miracle Hill Golf Course.

THE IRISH

"Arnold Palmer and I played in the 1960 Canada [now World] Cup at Portmarnock in Ireland, which was quite a big deal at the time," Sam Snead recalls. "All the politicians and whatnot came out, and there were a lot of speeches. The weather was unusually good, very bright and sunny with hardly any wind. Well, this old bird—I think he was the prime minister or something—says 'I want to personally welcome all of you American visitors to Ireland. As you can see, we are being blessed with typical Irish summer weather. In fact, this is the first typical Irish summer weather we've had in the past decade.'"

DON JANUARY

Don January walked slowly. He talked slowly. He swung the club slowly. Nothing ever seemed to bother him on the golf course.

During one tournament, CBS had Ken Venturi go over and ask January a few questions. When Pat Summerall, the anchor on 18, asked Venturi what January had to say, Venturi began laughing.

"Nothing," Venturi said. "I think he fell asleep."

BOBBY JONES

Given Bobby Jones's remarkable record, it is easy to forget how much he struggled and suffered in the early years of his career. That he would go on to win thirteen Majors overshadows the fact that it wasn't until the 1923 U.S. Open at Inwood that he finally won a national championship. At the depth of his despair, he turned to his good friend, writer O. B. Keeler, and asked, "Will I ever win a championship?"

Keeler, an older man who had carefully followed Jones's career, urged Jones to be both patient and confident.

"Bob, you're the greatest golfer in the world, and when you realize it, then you will win," he said.

Jones reached the finals of the 1916 Georgia State Amateur and faced Perry Adair, one of the finest young golfers in the South. Theirs was a celebrated rivalry, and the match attracted an enormous gallery.

Jones started badly and struggled on the greens for the first 18 holes. At the end of the morning round he found himself 3-down. After a quick lunch he retreated to the practice green to try to work out his putting problems. He'd been there for only a few minutes when the tournament chairman approached him.

"Bob, we've got an awful lot of people who've come out here to watch y'all," he said. "If the match ends early, would you mind playing out the bye holes?"

Jones was stunned.

"Don't you worry, sir," Jones said icily. "There won't be any bye holes."

Still furious, Jones hit a poor second shot on the first hole of the afternoon round. But from that point on, he was magnificent. He played the next seventeen holes in 2 under par and closed out the match on the final hole.

Like many talented young players, Jones had a fierce temper on the golf course.

In the 1916 U.S. Amateur at Merion, Jones, then just fourteen, met the 1906 champion, Eben Byers, in an early match. The clubs flew early and often. Finally, at one point, Byers became so incensed that he fired a club into the woods and refused to let his caddie retrieve it. Later, Jones laughed about his victory.

"I only won because Eben ran out of clubs," he said.

Five years later, Jones traveled to St. Andrews for the British Open. The course baffled him, and in the final round he lost his composure. After making double bogies on both the 10th and 11th, he tore up his scorecard and threw it into the wind. The British press, which would come to adore him, was merciless.

"Master Bobby Jones is a boy," one writer observed. "And alas, a rather ordinary boy at that."

Early on, Jones's temper was so ferocious and he was becoming so notorious that it very nearly cost him his playing career.

In the 1921 U.S. Amateur at the St. Louis Country Club, Jones faced British Amateur champion Willie Hunter in the second round of match play. With Hunter 1-up with two holes to play, he hit a fine pitch to the green. Jones, facing elimination, skulled his pitch. The ball raced over the green and into the thick rough. Incensed, he slammed his club to the ground. The iron bounced into the air and hit a woman spectator on the leg. She wasn't hurt, but Jones was humiliated.

The worst was yet to come. When he returned home to Atlanta, he received a stern letter from George Walker, the president of the USGA (and President George Bush's grandfather). The letter berated Jones and warned him that if he did not or could not keep his temper under control, he would be banned from all USGA competitions.

To his great credit, he responded to Walker and pledged to never again lose his temper in tournament play. As far as anyone can tell, he never did.

Jones faced a close friend, Watts Gunn, in the finals of the 1925 U.S. Amateur at Oakmont Country Club. Gunn and Jones were members at East Lake Country Club in Atlanta, and when they played at home Jones—who carried a plus-four handicap—would give Gunn three shots a side.

When they met on the first tee prior to the finals, Gunn asked Jones if he was "going to give me three a side today."

"No," Jones said. "I'm going to give you hell today."

And he did, beating him 8 and 7.

In 1930, Jones became the only American to win both the British Amateur and British Open in the same year. Upon his return to the States, he was given an enormous ticker-tape parade through the streets of Manhattan. Thousands turned out in the tremendous heat and humidity, and a phalanx of over fifty mounted policemen cleared the way for Jones's motorcade.

When he reached the steps of City Hall he was greeted by the mayor, the legendary Jimmy Walker. The irony of the situation wasn't lost on Walker.

"Here you are, the world's greatest golfer, being introduced by the world's worst one," Walker quipped.

Jones returned to Merion for the 1930 U.S. Amateur, the final leg in his Grand Slam. His routine was to arrive at the site of a Major championship several days ahead of time and play a series of practice rounds, first to familiarize himself with the course but also to round his game into shape. As a rule, he would not play on the day before the championship began, preferring to spend the day alone, reading one of the classics.

In 1930, however, America was mired in the depths of the Depression. This led USGA president Findlay Douglas and Robert Lesley, the president of Merion, to ask Jones if he'd play one last practice round. The reason? They needed the money. His previous practice rounds had drawn some 4,000 people a day—at $1 a head.

Jones was more than familiar with raising money for worthwhile causes. During World War I he played a series of exhibitions—most of them thirty-six holes a day—that raised over $150,000 for the American Red Cross. In many of those exhibitions he played with a childhood friend, Alexa Stirling, who had also learned the game from Stewart Maiden, the Scottish-born professional at East Lake Country Club. Jones and Stirling were known as the "Dixie Kids," and while Jones was the more famous of the two, Stirling was an outstanding player in her own right, winning the U.S. Women's Amateur—the biggest tournament in women's golf—in 1916, 1919, and 1920.

The 1930 U.S. Amateur was played not only during the Depression but also during America's most notoriously flawed attempt at social engineering—Prohibition. This led to an embarrassing moment for Bobby Jones.

Jones was checking into the fashionable Barclay Hotel in Philadelphia's Rittenhouse Square. There he would have a two-bedroom suite overlooking the Schuylkill River. On his way through the lobby, a bellman stumbled and dropped some of Jones's bags. There was the crash of breaking glass, and soon the sweet smell of corn whiskey filled the air.

Incidentally, the corn whiskey Jones favored was particularly potent. When Augusta National held its first members tournament, "corn" was served at both the 1st and 10th tees, in lieu of bootleg gin and whiskey, which was often raw bordering on poisonous. The problem was that many of the members—especially those from up north—were unfamiliar with just how potent corn whiskey could be. Let's just say there weren't a lot of low scores turned in that day.

If there has been one predictable—if regrettable—change in golf since the Jones era, it is the decline of the lifelong amateur. With the exception of marvelous players like Bill Campbell, Vinny Giles, Dick Siderowf, and a relative handful of others, most top amateurs can hardly wait to turn pro and take a shot at the Tour.

And who can blame them? The money is beyond belief, and that's where the best and truest competition exists. Jay Sigel, the greatest amateur of his generation, is a perfect case in point. After winning both the U.S. and British Amateurs and representing America on both the Walker Cup and World Amateur teams, he decided to try the Senior PGA Tour when he turned fifty. It wasn't the money. He was already a successful businessman. Instead, it was the lure of competition.

But in Jones's day, many of the top players remained amateurs—and lifelong friends. Fellow competitors like Francis Ouimet, Watts Gunn, Charlie Yates, and Jess Sweetser remained close to Jones throughout their lives. And while they were fierce rivals on the course, they regarded one another with considerable respect and affection. Witness this story from the semifinals of the 1930 U.S. Amateur at Merion.

Jones faced Jess Sweetser in the semis, and he knew he'd have his hands full. Sweetser had won the 1922 U.S. Amateur at The Country Club, beating Chick Evans, a former U.S. Open champion, in the finals. He had also won the 1926 British Amateur.

Jones jumped out to an early lead in the morning eighteen, but played indifferently in midround, as was sometimes the case when he established an early lead in match play. Still, by the end of the round he held a 4-up lead.

Jones won two of the first six holes in the afternoon, halving the other four. He then all but sealed the match by winning the 7th, 8th, and 9th to go dormie. On the 10th, both players hit fine drives. Sweetser's approach was hole high, but Jones knocked his very nearly into the hole. Sweetser conceded the match and the two friends walked back toward the clubhouse.

"Sweets, I feel kind of bad about that last shot," he said. "You know I wasn't trying to show you up or anything like that, don't you?"

"That's okay, Bob," Sweetser said. "I'd had enough by then anyway."

Francis Ouimet, who stunned the golf world by beating Harry Vardon and Ted Ray in a playoff for the 1913 U.S. Open at The Country Club, was easily one of the greatest amateurs of his time. Besides his Open triumph, he also won the 1914 and 1931 U.S. Amateurs.

Ouimet was a modest and mild-natured man. But on one occasion he lost his temper when a writer asked him why he went so long between U.S. Amateur victories. His answer puts Bob Jones's career into perspective.

"Bob Jones is the reason I didn't win the Amateur again until '31," Ouimet said. "You people have no idea of just how good he really was. None. He was more than just the greatest player of his day. He was as close as you could come to being unbeatable in this game."

Indeed, just look at his record in the U.S. Amateur. From the time he won his first Amateur in 1924 until he retired in 1930, he won five Amateurs and lost in the finals once.

Among all the attributes that made Bobby Jones a great competitor, one that is often overlooked is that he was a keen judge of human nature.

In the 1930 British Amateur at St. Andrews, Jones faced Great Britain's formidable Cyril Tolley in the second round. Tolley, the defending champion, was a two-time British Amateur champion and among the longest hitters of his time. Jones used this to his advantage.

Prior to teeing off, a friend mentioned Tolley's great length to Jones.

"Don't worry about Cyril," Jones said.

On the first hole, Tolley hit a long drive into the heart of the fairway. Jones blew it past him.

On the next hole, the same thing happened. Tolley, playing before a large gallery, began to press, trying to keep up with Jones off the tee. Soon he was overswinging and hitting the ball erratically.

Still, they had a fierce match, with Jones finally winning on the 19th hole.

When Jones retired from competitive golf after winning the 1930 British and U.S. Opens and Amateurs, many people were astonished. After all, he was only twenty-eight and the dominant player in the world. Still, those who knew him best knew the fierce toll that championship play took on him. British writer Bernard Darwin remembers seeing Jones following his final round in the 1930 British Open at Hoylake.

"I happened to be writing in the room where Bobby was waiting to see if he'd won," Darwin told a friend. "He was utterly spent, exhausted. He had to hold his glass with both hands, lest the good liquor spill. All he could say was that he would never, never do it again."

Bob Jones came from a comfortable background, but he was not, by any standard, a wealthy man at the time he was playing competitively. When he retired from championship play and returned to Atlanta, a group of his friends told him that they wanted to buy him a house in appreciation for all he had done to help put Atlanta on the map. They assured Jones that it was perfectly allowable under the USGA's Rules of Amateur Status.

Jones politely declined their offer. It violated his own set of rules.

Clearly, Jones knew better than most just how intense the pressures of competitive golf truly are. And he knew how much work it took to reach the top levels of the game. For those reasons, and because he knew how difficult it would be for his son to live up to his reputation, he was reluctant to see young Bob take up the game. But when the boy persisted, he arranged for him to get his first lessons from Stewart Maiden—the Scot who had molded Jones's game as a child at East Lake.

The practice session began early in the morning. At noon, young Bob laid down his club and headed for the clubhouse.

"Son, where are you going?" Maiden asked.

"To the clubhouse for lunch," he replied.

"I didn't say anything about lunch," Maiden said. "Come back here."

Practice—without a lunch break—lasted until twilight. Only then, with his hands sufficiently blistered and bloodied, could the boy return home.

In the years when Bob Jones played his best golf, there was no such thing as a matched set of clubs. Things like swing weights and frequency-matched shafts were light-years away. Players put together their sets purely by feel, and the best players had feel that was simply phenomenal. In Jones's case, it was almost eerie.

Years after he retired from competition, the A. G. Spalding company took his set of clubs and subjected them to a rigorous series of scientific tests. The results proved that the clubs all matched within extremely small tolerances. The exception was his mashie niblick.

"You know, I never could hit that club," Jones said when he learned the results of the test.

It is one of the ironies of golf history that following his competitive career, the game's greatest amateur was declared a "Non-amateur" by the USGA. The game's governing body determined that since Jones was making money from his line of Spalding golf clubs and from his instructional movies, he was no longer pristine enough to meet the strict standards of pure amateurism.

But in 1962 Joseph C. Dey, the wise and judicious executive director of the USGA, sent Jones an application for reinstatement of his amateur status. The application contained a number of questions, which Jones answered with tongue firmly in cheek.

Occupation: "Assistant."

Employer: "Clifford Roberts."

Do you understand the Rules of Amateur Status? "No."

Without mental reservations, have you decided to permanently abandon all activities contrary to the Rules of Amateur Status? "I have no mental reservations about anything."

After Jones had retired from competitive play, a writer who was interviewing him congratulated him on his utter lack of pretension. Jones looked at the man quizzically.

"Pretension?" he asked. "What in the world do I have to be pretentious about?"

As Jones grew older and the nerve disease syringomyelia gradually laid waste to his body, friends would delicately approach him with ways that he might be memorialized. Jones always politely declined, adding that Augusta National, the course he designed with Dr. Alister Mackenzie, "was memorial enough."

Jones died at home in the early evening of December 18, 1971, with his family by his side. Memorial services were private. In the spring of the following year, a Service of Thanksgiving and Commemoration was held at the parish church of the Holy Trinity in St. Andrews. Roger Wethered, whom Jones had beaten in the finals of the 1930 British Amateur, spoke for the millions who had been moved by the example of Jones's life.

"To have won through at golf after all those years when nothing would come quite right was an epic victory in itself, but the second victory—the one in which he was reduced to walking with a cane and, finally, to a wheelchair—was a victory of the spirit that will also live as long as his name is remembered."

TOM KITE

John Baldwin was a fine amateur golfer at the University of North Carolina in the 1960s. After graduating, he joined the PGA Tour and was playing in the 1967 Texas Open. He missed the cut, but this proved to be a great miss.

"I was going to leave for the next tournament, but a friend of mine convinced me to stick around," Baldwin remembers. "He said we'd go play in Austin with a couple of teenagers he said were pretty good players. We went out, and I absolutely played as good as I knew how to play. I shot a 67 and both of these kids beat me. That's when I realized it was time to quit the Tour and get on with my life."

He shouldn't have felt too badly. Those kids were Tom Kite and Ben Crenshaw—and in the end, it proved to be a good decision for Baldwin, who went on to a successful career on Wall Street and was a dominant amateur in the metropolitan New York area for many years.

TONY LEMA

Tony Lema, who won the 1964 British Open and died two years later in a plane crash, had a short but remarkable career. He joined the PGA Tour after a stint in the Marines and won eleven times. Still, given his background, it's a wonder he made it to the Tour at all.

He was born in desperate poverty in Oakland, California, and took up caddying to help make ends meet. A good athlete, he took a liking to the game and eventually gained enough confidence to enter a junior tournament in San Francisco. When he arrived at Harding Park, a municipal course, a woman took one look at his battered sneakers and started a collection to buy the kid a pair of decent golf shoes.

That woman was Ken Venturi's mother.

NANCY LOPEZ

It's often been said that no top athlete ever suffered fools more gladly than did Arnold Palmer, and that may well be true. But Nancy Lopez surely comes a close second.

One day she was on a flight when a man approached and introduced himself as one of her biggest fans. Then he asked if she ever watched *Star Trek*.

When she said that she'd seen it a few times, he pressed his hand gently to her face and held it there for a few seconds.

"It's a Vulcan Mind Meld," he explained. "I'm transferring your golf energy to me. I hope it helps."

Then he thanked her and walked away.

SANDY LYLE

It's unlikely that there's ever been a champion more down-to-earth and uncomplicated than Sandy Lyle, who won both the 1985 British Open and the 1988 Masters, as well as several other tournaments.

After his win in the British Open, he invited friends over to his house in Wentworth for a champagne reception the next day. After going through over eighty bottles of the stuff, he decided to go out for Chinese food—quite a lot of Chinese food. Not many newly crowned British Open champions would go get take-out for a crowd that large. And even fewer would do what he did after dinner.

The dishes.

DAVE MARR

Over the years, the late Dave Marr was occasionally criticized by writers for not being more critical of the players he covered, first on ABC and then NBC. The truth is, he wasn't afraid of calling a bad shot a bad shot. It's just that he had the ability to soften the criticism with his considerable sense of humor.

In one telecast, he watched as a player shot at a pin cut to the side of a green closely guarded by a pond.

"If that wasn't a pull, he's the bravest guy since John Wayne," Marr quipped.

If Marr was occasionally reluctant to be overly critical of players—especially struggling young players—it was because he never forgot what it was like to try to make it on tour when every dollar counted.

"I remember being in contention one year and I hit my approach shot into the water on one of the closing holes," Marr once said. "I thought, 'Well, David, you just drowned the mortgage payment.'"

The 1984 U.S. Open was played at Winged Foot Golf Club, where Marr had served as a young assistant pro under the legendary Claude Harmon. As part of its preview section for the Open, *Golf Digest* asked Marr to give a hole-by-hole description of the course. When he got to the difficult par-3 10th, he just shook his head.

"Man, when I was working for Claude I was in that right-hand bunker so often I had my mail delivered there," he joked.

Throughout his career, Dave Marr played in thousands of pro-ams and corporate outings. He always made it a rule to tell the amateurs not to be nervous.

"Trust me, there isn't a shot you can hit that I haven't seen before," he'd tell them.

Well, not quite.

In one pro-am, everything was going along nicely until they came to a par 3, and one of the players hit about as bad a shot as you can possibly hit. He laid the divot right over the ball.

"I take it back," Marr said. "That's a shot I've never seen before."

H. L. MENCKEN

The celebrated American journalist and humorist H. L. Mencken had a distinctively dim view of golf and the people who played it. In fact, the possibility of a golfer in the White House inspired Mencken to new heights of outrage.

"If I had my way, a man guilty of golf would be ineligible for any public office in the United States, and the families of the breed would be shipped off to the white slave corrals of the Argentine," he once wrote.

DR. CARY MIDDLECOFF

Anyone who has ever watched the Masters knows how quickly Augusta National can jump up and punish a player—particularly when it comes to the hard, fast, and severely contoured greens.

One year Doc Middlecoff, who won the 1955 Masters, hit a poor drive on the par-3 4th hole. The ball sailed over the green and came to rest in the thick hedges and shrubs. Middlecoff somehow managed to take a stance and then stabbed at the ball. Miraculously, it jumped in the air and came to rest some fifteen feet from the pin—but above the hole, a dangerous place to be on any green at Augusta.

"Man, I came out of there smelling like a rose," Doc said.

Four putts later, he left the green with a triple-bogey 6 and the bloom had gone off the rose.

JOHNNY MILLER

Even for a player as gifted as Johnny Miller, the pressure was intense when he went through the PGA Tour's Qualifying School.

To fight off the tension, Miller would retreat to his hotel room after dinner and swing a heavily weighted golf club. It built up his muscles, helped him groove his swing, and eventually tired him out enough that he could finally relax and get some sleep.

One night, however, things got a little weird. The club slipped from his hands in midswing. It crashed through a picture and then through the wall, and partially out the other side into a neighboring room—much to the surprise of the guest in the adjoining room.

The next day Miller earned his card and, much to his relief, was able to pay for the repairs to the room.

Almost everyone remembers Johnny Miller's remarkable 63 in the final round of the 1973 U.S. Open at Oakmont, but what's often overlooked is that he had to shoot it because of a near disaster in the third round.

Like many players, Miller kept a notecard with yardage and other jottings. In most cases, he would put the card in his golf bag after his round, but after the second round at Oakmont he took it back to the hotel. The next morning he left it in the room, and when he discovered his mistake on the first tee, he literally broke into a cold sweat. While he began the round in third place, he rapidly faded, going 5 over par for the first seven holes. In the meantime his wife, who had gone back to the hotel to get the card, was stuck in traffic for over an hour. Once she finally reached the course with the yardage card, Miller was able to settle down and play the last ten holes in even par. Still, he realized that if he was going to win the Open, he'd need a miracle round on Sunday.

He got it.

MOTHER ENGLAND

Edward, Duke of Windsor, is best known as the man who abdicated the British crown for Mrs. Wallis Simpson, the American divorcée whom he, as king, could neither marry, live without, nor keep tucked away as a mistress.

But Edward was a passionate golfer who, since he wasn't yet weighed down with either kingly duties or anything approaching a real job, had plenty of time to play. On a trip to Egypt in 1928, the prince decided that he must hit a drive from atop one of the Great Pyramids. What a sport. With his collection of lackeys and hangers-on applauding madly, he climbed to the top and played away.

And to think, there are people who, to this day, wonder why the British lost their empire.

The Duke liked to spend time with the other society swells in Palm Beach and enjoyed playing at Seminole with his friend, Chris Dunphy.

One time Dunphy invited the Duke and Duchess to come for dinner. When they accepted it presented an awkward problem for the Dunphys, since they had houseguests—Mr. and Mrs. Ben Hogan. For some reason—it couldn't have been a very good one—the Hogans weren't invited to the dinner.

The Duke and Duchess arrived at the appointed hour, and after meeting the other guests, the Duke took Mr. Dunphy aside.

"Where's Ben?" the Duke asked. "I was hoping to talk about golf with him."

After Nick Faldo decided to move to the United States and play the PGA Tour virtually full-time, a British writer asked him if there was anything he missed about living in England.

"A bit of rain now and again," Faldo replied.

BYRON NELSON

Byron Nelson is widely credited with developing the "modern" golf swing, but he also had a hand in two other innovations—the golf umbrella and an improved design for golf shoes.

Nelson was the professional at the Inverness Club in Toledo, Ohio. He became friendly with one of the members, Cloyd Haas, who owned a company that made umbrellas. One night over dinner, Byron asked Mr. Haas if his company, Haas-Jordan, couldn't develop a large, sturdy umbrella for golfers. Haas thought about it and asked Nelson to come to his factory and help develop the design for a golf umbrella. The umbrellas were a huge success, and Byron eventually became a vice president for marketing. In this role, he would visit major department stores during Tour events and call on executives, who were thrilled to meet the famous golfer. He was paid $25 per visit plus a year-end bonus—a profitable arrangement for everyone involved.

His involvement in the golf shoe business developed in much the same manner. One day, following a round at the old North and South Open at Pinehurst, he and his friend Jug McSpaden struck up a conversation with a salesman from Field and Flint, a shoe manufacturer.

Nelson asked the man why they couldn't design a shoe with a thicker sole that was sturdy enough to hold up in wet weather. The man arranged for them to visit the factory and consult on the design. "Foot-Joy" soon became the dominant golf shoe company, and Nelson and McSpaden received a royalty on each pair sold.

JACK NICKLAUS

When Jack Nicklaus was a small boy his father, Charlie, arranged for lessons with Jack Grout, the professional at Scioto Country Club.

Unlike a lot of today's teachers who have a gazillion cosmic theories about the golf swing, Jack Grout believed in keeping things as simple as possible, especially when it came to kids.

First, he thought they should hit the ball hard. Obviously, young Jack could do that.

Second, he insisted that they should keep their head steady through the swing. That proved to be a little more difficult for Jack—until Grout came up with a solution.

He told Jack to address a ball and then grabbed on to a handful of his crew-cut blond hair. Now, when Jack moved his head, it hurt. Sometimes it hurt a lot.

Nobody ever said improvement was painless.

When Jack Nicklaus won the 1959 U.S. Amateur, he earned an invitation to the 1960 Masters. While his friends around Columbus knew just how good Jack really was, for most of the people at Augusta he was just another very good amateur. Once they figured this out, Jack's friends found a way to make some money betting on Jack.

The bet worked like this: You take any twenty players in the field. We'll take Jack. If any of your players beat Jack, we'll pay. If Jack beats your guys, you pay—$10, $20, $50, take your pick.

It proved to be a memorable first Masters for Jack, and a profitable one for his friends.

L ong hitters have always drawn the biggest galleries, and that, in no small part, explains the popularity of players like Tiger Woods and John Daly. But if you talk to people who saw the young Jack Nicklaus play, they'll tell you that, given the equipment and course conditions of the time, he was every bit as long.

When he was in his twenties, he routinely drove the ball between 280 and 300 yards with remarkable accuracy. In fact, he was so powerful as a youngster that he would crush the face inserts of his driver. In 1961, the year he won his second of two U.S. Amateurs, he had to have the inserts replaced nine times.

One of Jack Nicklaus's greatest rivals during his amateur years was Phil Rodgers, a native of southern California who developed his considerable short-game skills under the eye of two-time PGA champion Paul Runyan. Rodgers won the 1958 NCAA Championship and made it to the quarterfinals of the 1957 U.S. Amateur.

Nicklaus came to the 1960 U.S. Amateur at St. Louis Country Club as the defending champion and odds-on favorite to win again, based in no small part on his second-place finish at the U.S. Open two months earlier.

If Rodgers thought Nicklaus was the favorite, he wasn't willing to admit it. In fact, he openly talked about how anxious he was to meet Nicklaus in match play. He told anyone who would listen that he would easily handle Nicklaus. One person who heard him was Nicklaus's biggest fan, his father, Charlie. The elder Nicklaus wasted no time telling his son about Rodgers's prediction—news that fueled Jack's already considerable competitiveness to the point where beating Rodgers became a singular fixation.

Nicklaus and Rodgers met on Tuesday morning and Nicklaus buried him, finishing 8 under par on the twelve holes they played before the match was closed out. It was an awesome performance.

Unfortunately for Nicklaus, he suffered a complete letdown in his afternoon match against Charlie Lewis and was beaten—as unlikely as this might seem—5 and 3.

Winged Foot's West Course is one of Jack Nicklaus's favorites. In fact, he had heard so much about it that he went out of his way to play it on his honeymoon.

When he arrived for the 1974 U.S. Open, a writer asked him if the course's finishing holes were among the best he'd ever seen.

"Yes," Jack said. "All eighteen of them."

Standing on the 18th tee in the final round of the 1967 U.S. Open, Jack Nicklaus seemed virtually certain to win his second Open. Even after he pushed his drive into the rough, his four-shot lead over Arnold Palmer looked insurmountable.

Studying his lie, he decided to play safe and pitch out short of the water. Maybe the shot was too easy or the lead too large. Whatever the reason, he stubbed the shot, barely advancing the ball.

Embarrassed, he said to Palmer, "What a dumb shot."

"You said it," Palmer replied. "I didn't."

When Jack Nicklaus arrived at Oakland Hills for the 1996 U.S. Open, he attracted the attention of Michigan's most famous—or infamous, depending on your point of view—physician, Dr. Jack Kevorkian, the advocate for assisted suicide.

"I just wanted Jack to know that if he missed the cut, I'm here," the good doctor said.

Like Bob Jones before him, Jack Nicklaus well understood the pressures and scrutiny his children would face when and if they took up golf. That was particularly true when it came to his oldest child, Jack Jr.

One day when Jackie was ten or so, he and his dad were playing. Jackie hit a poor shot and, as kids are wont to do, displayed a flash of temper. His father told him to knock it off, and when, a few minutes later, Jackie lost his temper again, his father had seen enough. They walked in.

It may not have been the last time Jackie let his temper get the best of him, but it was almost certainly the last time it happened in front of dear old dad.

By the way, Jack Nicklaus Jr. went on to become a fine player, winning the prestigious 1985 North and South Amateur as his parents looked on proudly.

One of the things that made Jack Nicklaus's win in the 1986 Masters so special was that his oldest son, Jackie, was caddying for him. When Jack putted out on 18, the two men embraced.

"Dad, watching you play today was the thrill of my life," Jackie said, as tears welled up in their eyes.

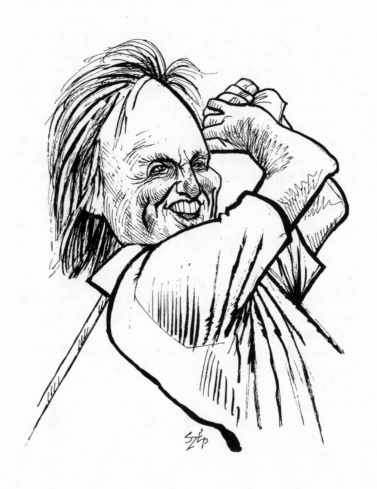

GREG NORMAN

For much of 1985 and 1986, Greg Norman was ill, nauseous, and weak. After a variety of tests, one doctor diagnosed Norman as suffering from an allergy to grass.

"It could be worse," he told the doctor. "I could be allergic to beer."

As it turned out, he wasn't allergic to either. Instead, he had walking pneumonia.

All but lost in the glow of Jack Nicklaus's 1986 win at the Masters was another of Greg Norman's close calls at Augusta National. Both he and Tom Kite came to 18 with a chance to tie Nicklaus but came up just short.

While it was another painful loss for Norman, he was delighted for Nicklaus. And while all the other players left, he stayed at the club until he had a chance to personally congratulate his friend.

ON THE ROAD AGAIN

In 1963 a man named Floyd Rood, who apparently had too much spare time on his hands, decided to go play golf—all the way from the Pacific coast to the shores of the Atlantic. Thirteen months, 114,737 strokes, and over 3,000 lost balls later, Floyd Rood finished—and presumably headed for the nearest bar.

Just after Christmas a few years ago, a man and his wife went to Hawaii for a golf vacation. When they got to the golf course the first day, she surprised him with a belated present: a dozen balls embossed with his name and the name of their home course.

Naturally, the grateful husband teed up one of the balls on the 1st hole, and promptly launched it out of bounds. Way out of bounds. So far out of bounds that he didn't even bother to look for it.

A few weeks after they returned home, the man received a package at his club. Inside was his ball, a photograph of a car, and a bill for replacing the glass he'd broken with his errant tee shot.

The old "Shell's Wonderful World of Golf" series took the game's best players to some of the most exotic locales around the globe—sometimes with unexpected complications. "One year we went to Guatemala for a match between Gardner Dickinson and Mason Rudolph," remembers Fred Raphael, the executive producer for the series. "After we checked into the hotel, Jimmy Demaret, who was one of our announcers, poured himself a drink and was looking out his hotel room window at the scenery. All of a sudden there was a roar and a nearby volcano erupted. Jimmy called my room and said, 'Fred, either they have the best damn whiskey in the world here in Guatemala or I just watched the top come off one of their mountains.'"

FRANCIS OUIMET

The 1925 U.S. Open was played at Worcester (Massachusetts) Country Club in oppressive heat and humidity.

After finishing one of his early rounds, Francis Ouimet, the winner of the 1913 Open, told a friend he wasn't sure he could play under such horrible conditions. The friend, who had just returned from a tour of Africa, said he had the perfect solution. The next day he met Ouimet at the course with a pith helmet and several large lettuce leafs he had soaked in cold water. He told Ouimet to place the lettuce on his head and then put on the helmet. Ouimet was skeptical but agreed to give it a try.

Francis Ouimet may not have been the most stylish person at the Open that week, but it turned out he was one of the coolest.

ARNOLD PALMER

When Arnold Palmer was a boy, his father, Deacon, was the professional at the Latrobe Country Club near Pittsburgh. Even though everyone loved young Arnold, there were restrictions on what he could do.

While he had won the club's caddie tournament four times, he was never allowed to receive the trophy or play in the other club tournaments. And while his friends could swim in the club's pool on hot summer days, Arnold did all his swimming in a stream that ran through the course.

Maybe it shouldn't surprise anyone that years later, when he was rich and famous, Arnold Palmer came back home to Latrobe and bought the club.

After dropping out of Wake Forest University, Arnold Palmer joined the Coast Guard hoping to be stationed in Florida so he could work on his golf game all year round.

He wound up in that noted seaport, Cleveland.

But Cleveland turned out to be a blessing. Palmer soon made friends with some of the top golfers in the area, who helped him get on some of the better courses. He also met a fine golfer and lawyer named Mark McCormack.

Back in the 1950s, the idea of a sports agent was almost an alien concept. Sure, Fred Corcoran would book outings for Sam Snead and Babe Zaharias and a few other golfers, but that was about the extent of it. But McCormack looked into the future and saw the enormous potential for athletes in general, golfers in particular, and one golfer specifically—Arnold Palmer.

McCormack began by handling a few small endorsement deals for Palmer, which was fine because Arnold was more interested in winning tournaments than reading the fine print in contracts. But soon, as Arnold became "Arnie" and the sheer volume of deals increased, it became clear that the two men would need to formalize their relationship.

"It was 1959 and Mark thought we should expand his role," Palmer explained. "He told me what he wanted to do, we shook hands, and I said, 'It's a deal.'"

In the years since, both men have become enormously wealthy—and they still have never had a contract.

When you've won as many tournaments as Arnold Palmer, it's easy to understand how a guy could sometimes make a simple mistake when it comes down to the small details.

Take the case of Royal Troon.

Palmer was playing a practice round prior to the start of the 1989 British Open at Royal Troon when a photographer approached and asked him to pose next to the plaque commemorating his historic win in 1961. Naturally Palmer, the most accommodating superstar in all of sports, agreed. The problem was, nobody seemed to know where the plaque was located. Finally, after several minutes, Palmer called over to his longtime caddie, Tip Anderson, and asked if he knew where the plaque was.

"Four hundred miles away," Anderson said. "We're on the wrong course."

Sure enough, there is a plaque honoring Palmer at Royal Birkdale, the site of his first British Open victory.

HARVEY PENICK

It's hard to imagine anyone wanting to pick a fight with Harvey Penick, or even being jealous of a man whose only goal in life was to help people get more enjoyment and satisfaction from the game of golf. Still, one day a fellow professional approached Mr. Penick and accused him of using his success as the coach of the University of Texas golf team to build his reputation as a teacher.

The man asked Mr. Penick if it was true that most of the kids who played for Texas were good players before they even arrived in Austin. Mr. Penick readily agreed. The man pressed on, asking if it was true that Ben Crenshaw already had made quite a name for himself before he left high school. Again, Mr. Penick agreed. Then the man went one question too far: he asked how good Ben Crenshaw was when he got his first lesson from Mr. Penick.

"Not that good, really," Mr. Penick said. "Of course, he was only about five years old back then."

Several years before Penick's death in 1995, *Golf Digest* sent an editor to Austin to interview him. The interview took place on a warm, sunny day on a patio at Austin Country Club. Joining in the interview were Tom Kite, Sandra Palmer, the winner of twenty-one LPGA events, including the 1975 U.S. Women's Open, and teaching professional Chuck Cook.

The interview occurred before the publication and phenomenal success of the *Little Red Book* series. Kite, Palmer, and Cook were happy to participate, because they hoped it would bring their teacher and friend some much-deserved national recognition.

There was only one problem with the interview: Mr. Penick was very soft-spoken and, by this point, very hard-of-hearing. This meant that the technician recording the interview had to turn up the volume loud enough to capture Mr. Penick's comments. Unfortunately, everyone else had to speak loudly enough for Mr. Penick to hear clearly. On top of all this, there were birds sitting in the nearby trees, screeching a high-pitched "Reeeet! Reeeet! Reeet!"

It turned out to be a fascinating interview—and a nightmare for the person who had to transcribe it.

PINE VALLEY GOLF CLUB

When the 1936 Walker Cup was played at Pine Valley Golf Club, it was an eye-opening experience for the members of the team from Great Britain and Ireland. They literally had never seen a course quite like it.

A member of the team stood on a tee and surveyed the great expanse of sand and scrub pine that stretched between him and the distant fairway.

"My God," he exclaimed. "Where are the bloody Indians?"

The Walker Cup is the supreme example of sportsmanship in golf. The players lucky enough to be selected to represent their countries forge bonds of friendship— among both their teammates and opponents—that last through the years. Two opponents in the 1936 Walker Cup teamed to write a poem describing their mutual feelings about Pine Valley:

We think that we shall never see
A tougher course than Pine Valley;
Trees and traps wherever we go
And clumps of earth flying through the air.
This course was made for you and me
But only God can make a three.

Ed Sullivan, the newspaperman who went on to become one of the biggest stars in the early days of television, was a passionate golfer. As a boy he had learned the game as a caddie along with one of his best friends, Gene Sarazen.

One day Sullivan drove to Pine Valley for his first round at the celebrated course. When he finished and repaired to the clubhouse, he was asked what he thought of the course.

"I know why it's called the Shrine of American Golf," Sullivan said. "People come here to have their games buried."

In 1950, a group of friends bet Bryan Fields, the general manager of Delaware Park Raceway, that he couldn't break 200 at Pine Valley. It seemed like a safe bet. Fields hadn't played golf in at least twenty years, and he'd be playing one of the hardest courses in the world with borrowed clubs and shoes. The initial bet was for $2,000, but with all the side bets factored in, the stakes were considerably higher.

Fields managed to shoot a 73 on the front nine, but when he made a 12 on the par-3 10th, his prospects dimmed considerably. Still, his caddie was optimistic. He told Fields that during the 1936 Walker Cup, a member of the Great Britain/Ireland team made a 17 on the hole.

"It could happen to anyone," the caddie said. "Don't give up."

With a charge worthy of Arnold Palmer, Fields rallied and closed with a 75 for a total of 148.

"See if I've been claimed," he called to friends as he triumphantly entered the clubhouse.

For all the frustration caused by Pine Valley's 10th hole, the all-time record for futility may be held by one John Brookes. He once took 44 strokes to play the 185-yard, par-3 14th hole. He walked to the 15th tee safe in the knowledge that things couldn't get any worse.

POLITICIANS

Former president Gerald Ford and the late, great Tip O'Neill were fierce political foes but the best of friends, in no small part because they shared a love of golf. Even after Ford had lost the presidency and Tip had retired as Speaker of the House, they still played a lot of golf together. Still, even though they were great pals, it didn't stop Tip from occasionally making a joke at his friend's expense.

"Geez, I love playing golf with Jerry Ford when we're in Palm Springs," Tip once said. "The problem is there's over fifty courses out there and I never know which one we're going to play 'til the President hits his first drive."

One day President Ford and Speaker O'Neill were paired together in the Bob Hope Desert Classic. When the President was introduced on the first tee, he got a respectful reception from the gallery, but when Tip was announced he was greeted with loud applause and cheers by a group just to the right of the tee.

A few minutes later, as President Ford prepared to hit his drive, the Speaker stopped him.

"Geez, Mr. President, be careful," Tip said. "There's a lot of Democrats over there, and we need all the help we can get."

It's a pretty good bet that no professional has played with more prominent politicians than has Sam Snead. One afternoon he played with then–Vice President Richard Nixon, and he got a revealing glimpse into the man who would go on to become the only president to resign from office.

"Well, Nixon wasn't what you'd call a good athlete, but he was a plugger," Sam explained. "I always thought he took up the game because Ike played. One day we're playing and the Vice President hit it off into the boonies. If he'd had a hundred Secret Service men with him, he couldn't have found that ball. I told him just take a drop, but he said he wanted to have a look. He's in there thrashing around. He might have gotten eaten by a bear, as deep in the scrub as he was. The next thing I know the ball came a-flyin' out of those trees. I told him it was a helluva shot, but he couldn't have gotten that ball out of there with a bazooka."

Like many of his predecessors, Bill Clinton often tries to escape the pressures of office by heading for the golf course. Whatever he may lack in skill, even his fiercest opponents will concede he more than makes up for in his passion and enthusiasm for the game.

Shortly after his reelection in 1996, he left for a visit to the Pacific. He planned a stopover in Hawaii that included—to no one's surprise—a little golf with an old friend, Hawaii former governor John Waihee. They planned to play a new course, Luana Hill Country Club, which was carved along the base of a volcano on the island of Oahu. It was a spectacular setting for a golf course, with towering palm trees and a staggering variety of tropical flowers.

Alas, the President never got to fully appreciate the course's natural beauty. Torrential rains arrived about the same time as the President, and the storms were unrelenting. Streams overflowed their banks. Fairways and greens were often under water. But the President played on—to the considerable amusement of the press corps, who credited the President with inventing a new game: "Aqua-golf."

That the President's visit was a washout didn't surprise many of the natives. They believed the course had been cursed.

It seems that back in 1985, when a group of developers set out to buy the land, the residents who were going to be displaced staged a series of protests—to no avail. One of the protesters, an elderly woman named Jennie Olinger, was forced to leave a banana patch she had tended for more than fifty years. As she left for the last time, she placed a curse on the developers who had taken her land.

Some ten years later, the curse kicked in and the rains came down.

Former vice president Spiro Agnew, who resigned in the face of federal corruption indictments in 1973, will never go down as one of America's great political leaders—or golfing politicians.

One day in a celebrity pro-am, he managed to hit three spectators with his first two drives. Just as he did when he resigned from office, Agnew figured the odds were against him and did the only logical thing: he quit.

When Franklin Roosevelt became president and began to enact his "New Deal" legislation, it angered many wealthy Americans. They called Roosevelt "a traitor to his class," which delighted him to no end.

But at least one group managed to get a measure of revenge against the President. When his son, Jimmy, was proposed for membership at the exclusive Los Angeles Country Club, the reaction was swift: he was blackballed and, for good measure, his sponsor was kicked out of the club.

THE PRESS

The late Charlie Price was a stylish and gifted writer. He was a keen observer of the game and a friend to generations of players dating back to Bob Jones and Walter Hagen.

In the early 1960s he collaborated with Bobby Jones on a book, *Bobby Jones on Golf*. Their routine was to work in the morning and then break for lunch, usually hamburgers that were brought to Jones's office. Before lunch they would have a martini. Sometimes a couple of martinis.

"You know, Charlie," Jones said one day, "I shouldn't drink these things. They interfere with my medicine."

"I know, I shouldn't drink them either," Price said. "They make me drunk."

Jim Gallagher Jr. comes from a golf family. His father is a PGA professional. His brother is a Tour pro. His sister is an LPGA pro, and his wife, Cissye, used to play on the LPGA Tour. Naturally, this made a good angle for writers working on pieces about Gallagher.

One day he was brought into the pressroom after his round

and was fielding questions. Everything went smoothly until a writer asked him a truly remarkable question.

"Jim," he asked. "What's your father's first name?"

In the long and storied history of the British Open, only two American amateurs have carried the trophy—the Old Claret Jug—back to America. The first, of course, was Bobby Jones. The second was Tony Wimpfheimer.

Before anyone goes searching the record books, an explanation is in order. Tony Wimpfheimer reigned for years as a vice president of Random House. Following his retirement he became increasingly active in the Metropolitan Golf Association, which serves the New York City area.

In the course of his career at Random House, he became good friends with Tom Watson. When Watson won the 1980 British Open at Muirfield, Wimpfheimer and his wife, Ann, flew back to the States with Tom and Linda Watson. When it came time to deplane, Watson took the magnum of champagne traditionally given to the Open champion. It was left to Tony Wimpfheimer to carry the ancient trophy off the plane—which he did gladly, realizing that it would provide a great story for hundreds of cocktail parties to come.

The late Henry Longhurst was not only a golf writer of considerable note but also a broadcaster who covered golf for the BBC, CBS, and ABC. Late in his career, he decided to walk away from television. His friend, British golfer-turned-announcer Peter Alliss, asked Longhurst why he was quitting.

"Having sucked the orange dry, I saw no reason to chew upon the pits," Longhurst said.

Over the years, professional golfers have enjoyed an amiable relationship with the writers who cover them. By and large, they have respected and trusted one another and cut each other plenty of slack. This, of course, does not include the members of the British tabloid press. Give them a sniff of scandal and they'll give you Page One headlines even more garish than the photos of the Page Three girls.

Generally, the Tabs only deign to cover the big golf events—the British Open or a Ryder Cup. If a scandal happens to coincide with one of these, so much the better. That was the case in 1995 when rumors spread that Nick Faldo's second marriage was headed down the slippery slope. Making things even merrier was the suspicion that there was a blond, American college student at the heart of the story. The Tabs were in heaven, but the players were less than amused. At the Ryder Cup, the European team was greeted in Rochester with much fanfare and a pack of tabloid reporters in a full feeding frenzy.

When one writer asked Scotland's Sam Torrance—yet again—if he thought Faldo's romantic entanglements might be a distraction, he responded with typical Scottish brevity.

"Go play in traffic," Torrance said.

Several years ago Jim Murray, the gifted columnist for the *Los Angeles Times*, wrote a tongue-in-cheek piece comparing present LPGA members with their predecessors. In the old days, he wrote, some of the players wore fedoras and smoked cigars. Naturally, some of the LPGA members were not amused.

They were equally unhappy at a recent U.S. Women's Open when, during an interview with England's Caroline Pierce, a writer asked her which current players smoked cigars.

Chuck Will is the senior associate producer for CBS Sports' golf coverage, which means that he is largely in charge of the nuts and bolts of the operation. In this role, it helps that he has been around the game since hickory shafts and is blessed with a wonderful sense of humor.

When Billy Andrade got married, he realized he had a problem. Billy's wife, Jody, had a degree in economics, and while she wanted to travel with him, the thought of lolling around on verandas from coast to coast held almost zero appeal for her. But Billy Andrade is nothing if not resourceful, and he came up with a great idea: Jody is smart. Jody is personable. Jody could go to work for CBS. Billy talked to Chuck Will, who agreed to give her a try. Everything was fine until Jody Andrade reported for her first day of work in the glamorous world of network television.

"You want to work here?" Will growled when she introduced herself.

"Yes," she said.

"OK, you're hired," he said. "Now get me a cup of coffee."
Beautiful.

Woody Hayes, the legendary Ohio State football coach, must rank as one of the most unlikely golf correspondents of all time, but that was his role in the 1960 U.S. Open at Cherry Hills.

Hayes was a close friend of the Nicklaus family, and since he was in Colorado at the time, he decided to travel to Cherry Hills and watch young Jack, then a twenty-year-old student at Ohio State, in the first round. To Hayes's dismay, he discovered that the Columbus newspapers weren't staffing the Open. Hayes, whose temper was already legendary, got on the phone to the papers.

"Where the hell are the reporters?" he thundered. "Here are the notes from the 5th hole on. Now get somebody out here."

Every year at the Masters, the executives from Tokyo Broadcasting host an elaborate party at a house in West Lake, a development not far from Augusta National. One of the great attractions is the elaborate and seemingly endless supply of Japanese food.

One year a writer arrived toward the end of the party and made his way into the kitchen, where he sat at a table with several waitresses who were having a late dinner. After helping himself to a heaping plate of sushi, he struck up a conversation with one of the women, who he assumed was from Japan.

"How . . . long . . . have . . . you . . . been . . . in . . . the . . . United . . . States?" he asked, speaking slowly, since he assumed the woman spoke little English.

"Why, I've lived here all my life," she answered with a southern drawl that would have done any true Daughter of the Confederacy proud.

If it can be said that there are any rules in sportswriting, one of the oldest must be "no cheering in the press box." In other words, reporters are supposed to be impartial observers.

That rule has never really applied to golf. Perhaps it's because golf writers play the game themselves and can more easily relate to what the players are going through. More likely, it's because the players—especially the great players—have been such exemplary human beings. Certainly Jack Nicklaus fits that description.

In 1963, the twenty-three-year-old Nicklaus came to The Country Club in Brookline, Massachusetts as the defending U.S. Open champion. He had already won the Masters and two other tournaments that year and was given a good chance of retaining his title at the course that has been the site of so much golf history.

Nicklaus started poorly, making bogeys on the first three holes in the first round and finishing with a 76. Things actually went from bad to worse in the second round, and when he bogeyed the 18th hole for a 77, he had missed the cut by a stroke.

Another player might have angrily cleaned out his locker and left town, but Nicklaus went to the pressroom and patiently answered every question, even though he was furious with himself.

When he finished, the writers gave him a standing ovation. While there will always be a debate about who is the greatest player in history, writers and historians agree that there was never a player who was more gracious in defeat than Jack Nicklaus.

In the early 1950s, Bill Davis talked two friends, Howard Gill and Jack Barnett, into joining him in starting a new magazine, *Golf Digest*. Some twenty years later, they sold the magazine to The New York Times Company and Bill became a vice president with the company. But for all his other responsibilities, he always kept his hands on the magazine and in the game. In fact, one of his great joys came from meeting the new editors that came on board as the magazine grew into the largest golf magazine in the world.

Bill was frequently brilliant. He was always quirky. He was occasionally maddening, mostly because his mind raced along in a totally nonlinear way. In short, Bill could make you crazy without really trying.

One evening, as he neared his retirement from The New York Times Company, he attended a dinner for the editors of

Golf Digest and its sister magazines. Bill got up to speak, and in the course of his sort of rambling speech, he stressed that every writer needs a good editor.

"Even Hemingway would have been a better writer if I had edited him," Bill said.

"Yeah," one editor said to the person next to him. "But he would have committed suicide ten years earlier."

THE ROYAL AND ANCIENT
GOLF CLUB OF ST. ANDREWS

American visitors to Scotland are often taken aback by the locals' strict, even passionate, devotion to the rules of golf. For them, the notion of something like "winter rules" is totally anathema to the spirit of the game.

Take the case of the American who sent his first drive on Scottish soil sailing out of bounds. He promptly teed up another ball and hit it down the middle of the fairway.

"In America we call that a 'mulligan,'" the American said to his caddie. "What do you call it over here?"

"Lying three," the caddie said, lifting the bag to his shoulder and striding off the tee.

An American tourist arrived for a late-afternoon round of golf at St. Andrews, but as luck would have it, the only available caddie was a stooped, elderly man who had already worked one loop that day. The American was apprehensive and told the caddiemaster that he didn't think the old man was up to a second trip around the Old Course, particularly since the Yank wasn't a very good golfer. The caddiemaster assured him that the caddie had the endurance of a man half his age, so off they went.

Sure enough, the American struggled with the gusting winds and capricious bounces. He didn't come close to breaking 50 on the outward nine, and things didn't get any better after they made the turn. Finally, it got to be too much for the caddie, who simply reached into the gorse and retrieved yet another errant drive. He put the ball in the bag and started walking back to the clubhouse.

"I'm sorry," the golfer said. "I was afraid you wouldn't be able to make it all the way around."

"Oh, I'm fine, sir," the caddie said. "But you've had enough for one day."

A hacker from America came to St. Andrews and, far from being inspired by the birthplace of golf, proceeded to top, shank, and slice his way around the course, despite the best advice his caddie had to offer.

After teeing off on 18, the two men walked over the ancient stone bridge that crosses the Swilcan Burn. The American looked down and then told his caddie: "If that water was deep enough I'd throw my clubs in, dive in after them, and drown myself."

"That wouldn't be possible, sir," the caddie replied. "You couldn't keep your head down long enough."

THE RULES

One of the things that makes golf so special is the respect, even reverence, that the players hold for the rules. Still, that's not to say that there aren't times when players get a little frustrated with rules officials. Take the case of Simon Hobday.

Hobday, an easygoing South African who won the 1994 U.S. Senior Open at Pinehurst, once had an interesting conversation with an official.

"If I called you an SOB, would you fine me?" he asked.

"Probably," the official replied.

"Well, if I was thinking that you're an SOB, would you fine me?" he asked.

"No," the official replied. "How could I?"

"Good," Hobday said, with irrefutable logic. "Then I'm thinking you're an SOB."

Hale Irwin ran into an interesting rules question during the 1973 Sea Pines Heritage Classic. He hit a drive, then watched in disgust as it bounded into the gallery. Imagine his surprise when he discovered that the ball had somehow managed to wind up in a woman's bra. What was the right ruling?

Was the ball out of bounds? Yes, in a manner of speaking.

Was her bra a temporary immovable obstruction? You could make a good case for it.

Or how about ground under repair?

Whatever the arcane machinations of the rules, common sense eventually prevailed. The woman discreetly removed the ball and Irwin got a free drop.

By any standard, E. Harvie Ward was one of the world's best golfers—professional or amateur—in the 1950s. He won the U.S. Amateur in 1955 and '56 and was undefeated as a member of three Walker Cup teams. But he also found himself at the center of one of the most controversial rules decisions ever reached by the USGA.

In 1956 Eddie Lowery, Francis Ouimet's caddie in the 1913 U.S. Open and a member of the USGA's Executive Committee, found himself locked in a dispute with the Internal Revenue Service. A review of his records revealed that Lowery had been paying Ward's golf expenses—a violation of the Rules of Amateur Status. The USGA suspended Ward—the reigning U.S. Amateur champion—from competition for a year.

"When I saw all these guys with new equipment I knew they weren't all rich," Ward said later. "Somebody had to be helping them out. The USGA knew it. They were just making an example out of me because I was the Amateur champion."

Eventually Ward turned professional and established a reputation as an outstanding teacher.

Want to know when you're having a bad caddie day? Just ask Raymond Floyd. Playing in the 1987 Tournament Players Championship, Floyd nailed an enormous drive and then looked on in horror as it rolled into his golf bag—for a two-stroke penalty.

For almost as long as there have been golfers, there have been problems with slow play and calls for draconian actions to help prevent it. Of course, some solutions are more drastic—and more successful—than others.

In 1930 Cyril Walker, the 1924 U.S. Open champion, was warned about his slow play. When he didn't pick up the pace, tournament officials disqualified him and ordered him to leave the grounds. He refused. They insisted. He still refused to go, so they called in the police and had him arrested.

The Rules of Golf often trip up even the best and most meticulous players. Take the case of Deane Beman at the 1960 America's Cup match.

The America's Cup was a competition between the best amateurs from the United States, Canada, and Mexico, and the 1960 American team was awesome. It featured the likes of Jack Nicklaus, Charlie Coe, and Beman, who would win two U.S. Amateurs and a British Amateur before turning pro and eventually becoming commissioner of the PGA Tour.

Ordinarily, the Beman-Nicklaus team would be odds-on favorites to beat all comers, but in this foursomes match they lost due to a Beman oversight. Prior to the match, Beman had been trying out one of Charlie Coe's wedges, and when it was time to tee off, he absent-mindedly stuck it in his own bag. Five holes later, he discovered his mistake and he and Nicklaus suddenly found themselves 5-down for violating the fourteen-club limit.

Very often a rules violation isn't the result so much of ignorance but of simply not paying attention. Take the case of Americans Jim Holtgrieve and Doug Fischesser in the 1979 Walker Cup at Muirfield, Scotland.

At the 14th hole in a foursomes match against Peter McEvoy and Brian Marchbank, both Holtgrieve and McEvoy hit poor drives. The Americans found themselves in the left rough while their opponents were across the fairway in the right rough. Marchbank's second shot went just a few feet, but the Americans never saw him hit it. The Americans reached the green in four and assumed that the opponents were on in three. When McEvoy holed his twenty-footer, both Americans assumed it was for a 4 and a win, so Holtgrieve picked up his ball. The mistake cost them the hole and they eventually lost the match, 2 and 1. Still, the American side prevailed, 15½ to 8½.

Lee Trevino was playing in the 1982 Tournament Players Championship but not playing very well. In fact, he was on his way to one of his worst rounds of golf as a professional when he hit his ball into a deep, greenside bunker on the 8th hole—his 17th that day.

The ball was embedded in the sodded side of the bunker, allowing Trevino to take a drop under the Embedded Ball Rule. After he took his drop, the ball was still unplayable, so he dropped again. Finally, in complete anger and frustration, he picked up his ball and placed it on a little clump of turf. By the time he finished the hole, he had no clue what he'd made and neither did the group's scorer.

"Just put down an 'X,'" he told the lady. "It doesn't matter, because I'm out of here today."

The people who run the Masters, which is to say the members of Augusta National, tend to do things their own way—and occasionally that applies to interpreting the Rules of Golf.

In the 1970 Masters, Arnold Palmer went for the green in two on the par-5 2nd hole, but his shot wound up in a greenside bunker. Whether he had a poor lie or tried to get too much out of the shot, Palmer failed to get his ball out of the bunker. In anger, he slammed his club into the sand—which is usually good for a two-stroke penalty.

Not at Augusta. Not when it's Arnold Palmer.

Tournament officials ruled that since he wasn't improving his lie or testing the sand, there shouldn't be any penalty.

Some of his fellow competitors politely—and very quietly—disagreed.

The Rules of Golf strictly limit what amateurs can accept in prizes, and it most definitely doesn't include cash. So consider the dilemma faced by one Jason Bohn.

Back in 1992, the nineteen-year-old Bohn was playing in a charity golf event near his home in Alabama. He was one of just twelve participants invited to take a shot at a hole in one. The rules were simple. Each player got to hit one ball on a 140-yard par 3. Everyone failed, except Jason Bohn, whose hole in one earned him $1,000,000.

The problem was, if Bohn took the money he had to give up his amateur status.

Some problem.

In about one nanosecond, Jason Bohn turned pro and became one of 1992's leading money winners.

THE RYDER CUP

Virtually any discussion or article about the Ryder Cup inevitably comes back to the enormous pressure individual players feel when they compete for their country. This has been particularly true since the early 1980s as the European teams have gotten stronger and more successful. It's only natural to expect young players to feel the pressure, but it even affects some of the game's most successful players.

"I was paired with Hale Irwin in the foursomes in 1977," Lanny Wadkins remembers. "It was my first Ryder Cup, and since Hale had played in 1975 we planned to have him hit the first drive.

"We stood on the first tee, and Hale turned to me and said he didn't like the way the hole fit his eye. He told me to go ahead and hit it.

"In 1991, at Kiawah Island, we were paired together, and again the plan was for Hale to hit the first drive. We were on the tee waiting to be announced, and he turned to me and said, 'Lanny, I don't like the way the wind is blowing. I might not get it in the fairway. You go ahead and hit it.'"

Brad Faxon was a rookie member of the 1995 Ryder Cup team at Oak Hill Country Club. The United States held a two-point lead going into the Sunday singles matches, but the Europeans rallied and the matches tightened.

After Davis Love III closed out Costantino Rocca, 3 and 2, he raced to the 17th green to try to lend moral support to Faxon, who was facing David Gilford. As Faxon walked off the green, Love approached.

"Fax . . . " he said.

Faxon waited. No other words would come. Love was choking so bad, he couldn't even speak.

Faxon just shook his head, laughed, and headed for the next tee.

It shouldn't come as a surprise to anyone that Sam Snead has a remarkable Ryder Cup record. He played on nine teams and was the nonplaying captain in 1969. In the thirteen matches he played, he won ten, lost two, and tied one. In singles play he won six of the seven matches he played. As good as this record is, it could have been even better if it hadn't been for an almost comical violation of the rules.

In 1961, the forty-nine-year-old Snead had played well enough to qualify for the Ryder Cup team and planned to take a couple weeks off before leaving for the matches at Royal Lytham and St. Annes. Accordingly, he wrote officials in Portland, Oregon, saying that he wouldn't be playing in their tournament.

So far, so good. But then his old friend Ed Tutwiler, one of the country's best amateurs, asked Sam to be his partner in something called the Losantiville Pro-Am Championship in Cincinnati. Tutwiler figured he'd need a player of Sam's caliber if he was going to beat the defending champions—a kid named Jack Nicklaus and his college golf coach, Bob Kepler.

When Sam arrived at the course, a friend reminded him that as a tournament winner, he needed special approval from a PGA-sanctioned tournament to compete in what was deemed to be a competing event, according to the unusually arcane PGA of America rules. Sam sent a wire to the people in Portland asking for a waiver and then teed off.

After his round, he returned to the clubhouse and found he had received a wire from Portland saying that his request had been denied. Later in the day he received a second telegram, this time from the PGA, informing him that he'd been fined $500 and suspended from PGA-sanctioned tournament play for six months. In effect, he'd been kicked off the Ryder Cup team—the same team he'd captained in 1959.

Sam told the PGA that he planned to appeal the ruling. The PGA said they'd take up the appeal at their annual meeting. Following the appeal, Sam's suspension was reduced to forty-five days. Of course, this was small comfort. The annual meeting was held after the Ryder Cup competition.

"It was the worst slap in the face I ever had," Sam said years later.

It may be hard to believe, given the Ryder Cup's enormous popularity today, but as late as 1975, the organizers had to scramble to drum up any publicity they could get.

The 1975 Ryder Cup was played at Laurel Valley Golf Club near Pittsburgh. The United States hadn't lost the Cup since 1957, and you would have been hard-pressed to find anyone who thought they were going to lose this time around. Not with players like Jack Nicklaus, Tom Weiskopf, Lee Trevino, Raymond Floyd, Billy Casper, and Johnny Miller on the American side.

To help boost the lagging ticket sales, the PGA of America arranged for an exhibition match between the team captains, Arnold Palmer and Bernard Hunt, and entertainers Bob Hope and Perry Como.

Mercifully, it was rained out.

SHOW BUSINESS

Anyone who has ever watched one of W. C. Fields's movies knows what remarkable hand-eye coordination he had. He was a skilled juggler and masterful around a pool table. He was also a good golfer, and he appeared in one of the instruction films Bobby Jones made after his competitive career ended. True to form, though, Fields never let golf get in the way of his drinking.

"I always carry a bottle in my bag in case of an emergency," he once told a writer. "Fortunately, I also carry a snake in my bag in case I need to invent an emergency."

For many years, a prominent feature of the Bing Crosby National Pro-Am was Bing's Sunday night "Clambake." As the party wore on and the alcohol flowed freely, Bing would eventually take the stage and sing a few of his favorite songs.

Everything was going along smoothly at the 1960 Clambake. Bing was in fine voice and then, midway through his performance, there came a tremendous roar from the back of the room—where Johnny Weissmuller was swinging from a chandelier and giving his Tarzan yell at the top of his voice.

SAM SNEAD

In hockey, a "hat trick" is when a player scores three goals in one game. In the old days, fans would toss their hats down onto the ice in tribute to the player. Sam Snead scored a hat trick of sorts one year in Canada.

"We were playing this par 3," he recalls. "It was 245 into the wind, and most of the boys couldn't even reach the green. I took a driver and hit the prettiest little hook in there that you ever saw. The ball hit on the front of the green and started rolling like a putt. It ran up over a ridge, and I lost sight of it. When I heard the crowd roar I figured it was close, but when I saw them start throwing their hats onto the green, I knew it was a hole in one."

A writer once asked Sam which pair of brothers had the most wins on tour.

"Jay and Lionel Hebert?" Sam guessed.

"No," the writer said.

"Ed and Marty Furgol?" Sam asked.

"Nope," the writer said.

"Then it's got to be Lloyd and Ray Mangrum," Sam said. "That Lloyd was a hell of a player."

"Nope," the writer said. "You and Homer."

"By God, you're right," Sam said, a smile breaking across his face. "And Homer only won once."

Because Sam played so well for so long, he had a chance to compete against players who were the same age as his sons. While Sam was intensely competitive and rarely gave the other guy an edge, he did give some of these young players a bit of advice from time to time.

One day a young player asked if he could join Sam for a practice round. Sam agreed and, just to make things interesting, a little bet was made on the round. After a few holes, Sam took the player aside.

"Son, don't call anyone you're trying to beat 'Mister.'"

Sam Snead grew up in the small town of Hot Springs, Virginia, in the shadow of the famous Homestead Hotel. One day when he was seven, Sam wandered away from home and found himself at the Homestead, where a woman asked him if he'd like to caddie for her. He wasn't quite sure what being a caddie entailed, but when he learned he could earn a little money, he was all for it.

Off he went with the woman, and when they finished she took his hat and filled it with pennies and nickels.

151

"I looked real hard for a dime, but there wasn't one," Sam said.

With a new job and a hat full of money, Sam set off for home, a two-mile walk. When he got there he could hardly contain himself.

"Look Mom," he said, proudly holding his hat out for her to see his riches. "I earned all this money caddying, Mom, and it's all for you."

What was her reaction?

"She was real pleased to see that money," Sam recalls. "But that didn't stop her from taking that switch out from behind her and giving me a good licking for wandering off and scaring her half to death."

LEFTY STACKHOUSE

"People are always writing about old Tom's temper, but let me tell you something, I'm not even close to Lefty Stackhouse," Tommy Bolt once told a writer friend. "Lefty was playing in a pro-am down in Texas one time, and he and his partner were doing just fine until they came to this one hole. Lefty's ball was just off the green, but his partner was close to the hole and looking at a birdie, so Lefty picked up. His partner three-putted for a bogey, and Lefty got so damn mad he punched himself in the head. He started bleeding so bad, he had to go back to the clubhouse and get himself bandaged up. Old Lefty was a beauty, that's for sure."

CURTIS STRANGE

It's often said that twins have an almost psychic ability to communicate and understand what their sibling is going through. That may well be true. Take the case of Curtis Strange and his twin brother, Allen.

When Curtis beat Nick Faldo in a playoff to win the 1988 U.S. Open, he was understandably excited. So excited, in fact, that he couldn't get to sleep. Not wanting to wake his wife, Sarah, he called Allen at four in the morning. He apologized for calling at that hour.

"That's OK," Allen said. "I couldn't sleep either, and I was thinking about calling you."

TEMPER, TEMPER

Clayton Heafner was a fine player. Like many fine players, he fought a hook. And he fought his temper. Very often, the hook and the temper managed to win.

"Clayton could really play, but every so often that old right hand of his would take over and he'd hit some of the ugliest hooks you'd ever hope to see," Sam Snead remembers. "He was leading a tournament one time when he hooked one out of bounds. You could just tell he was going to explode. Damned if he didn't walk over to this tree and punch it. I think he broke his hand, too."

"I was playing in an outing one day and I saw a guy absolutely lose it," Dave Marr once recalled. "It was one of those deals where I stood on a par 3 and hit a shot for each group. This guy gets up there and dead shanks it into a pond next to the tee. Man, you could just see the red come up into his face. He took his club and threw it into the pond, then he reached over, picked up a golf bag, and threw that in, too.

People were in shock. I said, 'I can't believe you did that.' One of the other guys said, '*You* can't believe it! It was my bag!'"

Ky Laffoon possessed a temper that is by now the stuff of legend. Most of the stories about him deal with some damage he did to either himself or one of his clubs that somehow offended him. But in the 1938 Masters, he took out his anger on an unsuspecting spectator.

Laffoon was paired with Henry Picard in the final round, which was being played on a Monday due to rain earlier in the week. With Ralph Guldahl and Harry Cooper in the clubhouse with scores of 287, Picard appeared to be the last man on the course with a chance at winning.

On the 15th hole, Picard hung his approach shot out to the right. It bounded into the gallery, where it struck a spectator's cane and ricocheted into some shrubs. Picard played a good pitch and was able to salvage his par. As he headed for the 16th tee, he heard a commotion back in the gallery—Laffoon had the spectator by the throat.

"Do you realize you could have cost that man the tournament if his ball had gone in the water?" Laffoon screamed, the veins bulging in his neck.

Picard, by the way, went on to win by two strokes despite all the excitement.

LEE TREVINO

Before the Senior Tour really took off, a writer asked Lee Trevino if he had any goals for when his playing days were over. Trevino thought about it for a second.

"When I turn sixty I'm going to get me one of those old blue blazers, sprinkle it with dandruff, spill some soup on my tie, and then go run the USGA," he joked.

Lee Trevino's place in golf history is secure, if only for his record against Jack Nicklaus. Nicklaus finished second in four of the six Major championships won by Trevino. Trevino began by beating him at the 1968 U.S. Open at Oak Hill and then beat him again in a playoff to win the 1971 Open at Merion. By 1972, when Trevino chipped in for a par on the 71st hole at the British Open at Muirfield, it had become too much for Nicklaus to bear.

"You've done this too many times," Nicklaus said as he congratulated Trevino on his win. "Why don't you go back to Mexico."

For several years, Lee Trevino skipped the Masters. He believed that Augusta National was ill-suited to his game because he wasn't a high ball hitter and didn't feel comfortable drawing the ball. Also, he never really felt comfortable at the club.

In 1971, he decided to take Masters week off but at the last minute decided he wanted to play—just not at Augusta. So he entered a PGA sectional tournament in El Paso.

To no one's surprise, he won the tournament and the princely sum of $125.

HARRY VARDON

England's Harry Vardon, winner of six British Opens and the 1900 U.S. Open, was a man of few words who did not suffer fools gladly. It's easy to imagine, then, how testy he might have become at times during a promotional tour of the United States. Vardon was a genuine celebrity, even in a country where golf's appeal was in its infancy.

During one stop on his tour, a new golfer asked Vardon if he consciously tried to keep his left arm straight on his backswing.

"No," Vardon said.

"Do you think it's important for a beginning golfer to keep his left arm straight?" the man asked.

"No," Vardon said. "As a matter of fact, I rather like playing against people who insist upon keeping their left arm straight. I find that they seldom think of anything else."

KEN VENTURI

No amateur has ever won the Masters, but Ken Venturi came close in 1956, when he led going into the final round.

At that time, it was a tradition that Byron Nelson played with the leader on the last day. That presented a problem.

"Cliff Roberts came up to me Saturday night and said that since Byron was my mentor they thought it would be better if I didn't play with him in the last round," Venturi recalls. "Nobody thought Byron would coach me or anything, but they didn't want my win to be tainted in any way. He told me I could play with anyone else I wanted. I thought about it and decided I wanted to be paired with Sam Snead. I figured that since I'd learned from Byron and polished my game with Ben Hogan, what could be better than playing with Sam when I won my first Major."

Roberts tried to dissuade Venturi.

"He said it was up to me, but he thought Sam could be tough," Venturi remembers.

The final round was played in windy, difficult conditions. Venturi continued to play well from tee to green, but his putting failed him and he finished second behind Jackie Burke, who was the only player to break par in the last round.

When he returned home to San Francisco, a newspaper reported that Venturi had been critical of the way Snead treated him on the course. Naturally, this caused an uproar at Augusta National and throughout the golf world, even though Venturi insisted that the quotes were inaccurate. Some twenty years later, he put the issue to rest.

The occasion was a black-tie dinner at the Waldorf-Astoria hotel in New York. Both Snead and Venturi were being honored, and when Venturi rose to speak, he recounted the painful last round of the 1956 Masters. He spoke movingly of how he struggled to maintain his composure as the tournament slipped from his grasp. Then he turned to Sam.

"After the tournament, a newspaper reported that you gave me the treatment in the last round," he said. "That's not true. You went about your business and let me go about mine. That's as it should be. I wanted to play with you because I felt that, if I was lucky enough to win the Masters, it would be an honor to walk up the 18th fairway at Augusta with you. And I want to say this right now for the record: if I had to do it again, I'd still choose you, Sam."

One of the cardinal rules of golf is that you should always focus on the present. Don't worry about the shots you've already played. You can't get them back. And don't think about the future, either. It was a rule that Ken Venturi broke on the last day of the 1956 Masters.

"A friend came up to me before the round and congratulated me," Venturi remembers. "He said that if I won as an amateur, I'd get enough business offers that I'd become a millionaire. It was funny, but I started thinking about the new house I'd be able to buy for my parents. I knew I shouldn't think that way, but I couldn't help myself."

Venturi never did win the Masters, although he did finish second again in 1960. By 1964, he was on the verge of quitting the Tour. He had suffered injuries in a car accident that continued to nag him. His marriage was falling apart. He was all but broke, and the man who was once one of the game's brightest stars had to routinely swallow his pride and ask for sponsor's exemptions into tournaments. It was one such exemption that set the stage for his win in the 1964 U.S. Open and one of the greatest comebacks in sports.

"Westchester was right before the Open, and I desperately wanted to play there because the course is very similar to the way Open courses are set up," Venturi says. "I called Bill Jennings, who owned the New York Rangers, and asked him if there was any way he could get me an exemption. I told him I really believed that my game was finally coming around. He said he'd see what he could do. He called me the next day and told me I was in."

Venturi played beautifully. On the last day, he gambled and made a clutch par on the long, dangerous par-3 16th, then birdied 17. He finished third, and while it wasn't a win, it was the next-best thing. Ken Venturi, the man who had tasted greatness, found an isolated corner of the locker room and sobbed the tears of a man who had finally stared down defeat.

Few people gave Ken Venturi much of a chance at the 1964 U.S. Open. Even after the first two rounds, he found himself six shots behind the leader, Tommy Jacobs, and five behind the pretournament favorite, Arnold Palmer. Worse yet, people wondered how Venturi, still bothered by injuries, would fare over thirty-six holes of heat, humidity, and pressure on the last day of the Open.

But on the first hole of his morning round, Venturi found cause for hope.

"I hit my approach about twelve feet from the hole," Venturi says. "I hit a good putt, but the ball hung right on the lip. I remember just staring at the ball as hard as I could, willing it to drop into the cup. As I walked up to the hole, it fell. I said to myself, 'Okay, you've got one shot to play with. Shoot at every flag until you give it back.'"

Venturi went out in thirty and shot a 66 that put him two shots behind Jacobs going into his afternoon round—and set up one of the most courageous victories in U.S. Open history.

Ever since he took up the game as a kid, Roger Maltbie has been a huge Ken Venturi fan. In fact, he went to an exhibition Venturi held early in 1964 and asked him for an autographed ball.

Does he still have it?

"No, I was going to play in a junior tournament and I didn't have any decent balls, so I took the one Ken gave me, wiped his name off, and played with it in the tournament. A couple weeks later, he won the Open. Shows you how smart I am."

Ten years after his win at the U.S. Open, Ken Venturi came to Winged Foot to play in the 1974 Open. Beset by injuries, he was only playing the Tour sporadically, devoting most of his time to his work as a commentator for CBS Sports.

He struggled at Winged Foot and was never really in contention. As he trudged up one of the final fairways, a man in the gallery said to a friend, "If I was him I'd quit."

"Yeah," the friend replied. "But if you were him, you'd have quit ten years ago, too."

THE WALKER CUP

In the 1930 Walker Cup at Royal St. George's Golf Club, American Donald Moe staged one of the greatest comebacks in the history of the competition.

After falling 7-down to Bill Stout, he fought back and finally won the match with a birdie on the 18th hole.

"That was not simply golf," said Stout following the match. "That was a visitation from the Good Lord himself."

In 1932, the Walker Cup came to The Country Club in Brookline, Massachusetts. To commemorate his historic win there in the 1913 U.S. Open, Francis Ouimet was named as the captain of the American team. That was certainly newsworthy. The United States won, 8–1, and three matches were halved. That was newsworthy as well. But the big news was that the matches were temporarily halted due to darkness when there was a total eclipse of the sun.

Sportsmanship has always been at the heart of the Walker Cup, and one of the best examples of this occurred in the 1953 matches at The Kittansett Club in Marion, Massachusetts.

James Jackson of the United States was playing in a foursomes match when, to his horror, he discovered that he had sixteen clubs in the bag and faced a penalty that would have cost the match.

His opponents wouldn't hear of it and insisted on winning by virtue of their play. As luck would have it, the United States won this match, as well as the Walker Cup, 9–3.

The 1965 Walker Cup match at the Five Farms Old Course of the Baltimore Country Club ended 11–11 with two matches halved—the only tie in the history of the competition.

The entire gallery, as well as both teams, gathered on the 18th hole to watch the dramatic conclusion—the singles match between American Mark Hopkins and England's Clive Clark.

Hopkins came to the home hole 1-up, and it looked as if he would hold on and win the crucial point as Clark faced a thirty-five-foot putt for a win. It wasn't to be. Clark somehow made the putt, to the considerable relief and joy of his teammates and their supporters. No one was happier than Ireland's Joe Carr, the captain of the Great Britain/Ireland team.

"Your head moved and your body moved, but how in the world did you get the cup to move in the way of the ball?" he asked Clark.

The United States holds an enormous edge in Walker Cup victories, 31–4–1. One of those victories came in 1969, when the Americans won, 10–8, at the Milwaukee Country Club. There were six halved matches, and the U.S. won several matches with clutch play on the 17th and 18th holes.

After the match, America's Vinny Giles tried to console Britain's Michael Bonallack.

"You know, if these had been sixteen-hole matches you guys would have been in great shape," Giles said.

"No," Bonallack said, sighing. "I think we would have found a way to screw up 15 and 16."

TOM WATSON

Tom Watson and Jack Nicklaus have enjoyed a wonderful rivalry over the years, dating back to their historic duel at Turnberry in the 1977 British Open. In 1982, when Tom Watson chipped in on the 71st hole of the U.S. Open at Pebble Beach, it allowed him to edge Jack Nicklaus—who was the first player to congratulate Watson when he walked off the final green.

Watson and Nicklaus were paired together in the second round of the 1991 Masters. Watson played his way into the lead that day, and as the two men approached the 18th green, the enormous gallery rose and gave the two a huge ovation. Watson slowed to let Nicklaus catch up.

"Go ahead, Tom," Nicklaus said. "You go first."

"No, Jack," Watson said. "Let's walk up together."

"But you're leading the tournament," Nicklaus argued.

"Yeah, but you're Jack Nicklaus," Watson said.

TOM WEISKOPF

The 1974 U.S. Open was played at Winged Foot Golf Club in Mamaroneck, a suburb of New York City. The week before the Open the Tour was in Philadelphia, and most of the players drove straight to New York when the tournament finished. Tom Weiskopf was one of them, although his route was a little more circuitous than most.

Before leaving Philadelphia, Weiskopf checked to make sure he had the directions to Winged Foot. So far, so good.

And he also had the directions from Winged Foot to the house he was renting in nearby Bronxville. Okay, fine.

What he didn't have were the directions from Philadelphia to Bronxville. So he did the only logical thing. He drove to Winged Foot, arriving at midnight. Then he checked the directions and drove on to Bronxville.

JOYCE WETHERED

When Joyce Wethered died in 1997 at the age of 96, the obituaries were fulsome in their praise.

The *Times* of London called her "the most stylish and successful woman golfer of her day, and is still widely regarded as the best the world has seen."

No less a figure than Bobby Jones was at least that impressed with Wethered. After the two played a 1930 exhibition at St. Andrews, Jones said he doubted that there had ever been a better golfer, man or woman.

Indeed, in 1950 when the Associated Press ranked the best golfers of the first half of the twentieth century, Wethered ranked first among women and seventh overall behind Jones, Ben Hogan, Walter Hagen, Byron Nelson, Sam Snead, and Gene Sarazen.

Lady Heathcoat Amory, as she became known following her 1937 marriage to Lord Heathcoat Amory, was largely self-taught. She learned the game by playing with her brother, Roger, who would go on to win the 1923 British Amateur. And like Jones and Nelson, hers was a relatively short but remarkable career. She won the British Amateur championship in 1922, 1924, 1925, and 1929 and also won four straight English Amateurs beginning in 1920.

She entered the 1920 English championship at the insistence of friends and, despite having taken just one lesson and having limited competitive experience, beat the formidable Cecil Leitch in the final. It was the first loss in a nonhandicap match that Leitch had suffered in seven years.

Lady Heathcoat Amory's swing was often described as technically perfect, and, with her remarkable balance and fluidity, she was able to hit the ball enormous distances. That she was unusually tall, 5'10", also helped.

"She could stand barefoot on a cake of ice and hit a ball 240 yards," said Scottish professional Willie Wilson.

Indeed, in an exhibition with members of a British Walker Cup team, she routinely drove the ball well past the men— to their considerable distress.

In 1925, at age 23, she stunned the British sporting world by retiring after winning the British Amateur.

She emerged from retirement to play in the 1929 British Amateur, where she met the great American champion, Glenna Collett, in the finals. Five-down after eleven holes of the thirty-six-hole match, Wethered rallied to win, 3 and 1.

After retiring for a second time, she went to work for a London department store advising people about golf clothes and equipment. The job brought her perilously close to being declared a professional under the strict rules of amateur status, but she removed all doubt by agreeing to appear in a series of exhibitions in the United States. Featuring the likes of Jones, Sarazen, and other top players, the exhibitions drew large galleries and earned Wethered over $20,000.

Following her first retirement from competition, she was asked by a baffled press why she would leave the game at the height of her considerable powers.

"I have simply exercised a woman's prerogative of doing something without the slightest regard for what anybody thinks, and because I want to please myself." she said.

Some people said she had spoken like a true woman.

The truth is, she had spoken like a true champion.

THE WILD KINGDOM

When the great British rugby star Gordon Brown was a youngster growing up near the Royal Troon Golf Club in Troon, Scotland, he once got the scare of his life.

He was walking home one night and decided to take a shortcut across the 11th hole. There, near one of the fairway bunkers, he saw an enormous brown bear. Young Jones raced home with the news—and was immediately punished for lying. Everyone knew there were no brown bears in Troon.

Well, almost none. It seems there was a traveling circus in the area and one of the star performers was a gypsy and his dancing bear—who spent their nights sleeping under the stars on the 11th fairway.

Back in 1987, a golfer was playing on a course that sat next to a military air base in the African nation of Benin. Naturally, this could prove to be a distraction for the golfers. However, in one case, a golfer proved to be a major distraction for the military.

It seems that a golfer hit a lovely, high drive. So high, in fact, that it struck a large bird flying overhead. The disoriented bird plummeted to earth and into the open cockpit of a fighter rolling down the runway, causing the pilot to lose control. The plane veered off the runway and crashed into a row of parked planes, causing them to burst into flame, spelling the demise of the entire Benin Air Force.

Billy Burke, the 1931 U.S. Open champion, had a pet dog named Jerry that was remarkably well-behaved. The dog would accompany Burke on practice rounds and would roam freely until it was time for Burke or one of his playing partners to hit. Then he would immediately stop and sit. The amazing thing about the dog is that he did this instinctively. Burke never had to teach him. He did it from the very first time Burke took him on a course.

WIVES, LOVERS, AND OTHER STRANGERS

O ne of the great and enduring love stories in golf is that of the marriage of 1928 U.S. Open champion Johnny Farrell and his wife, Kay.

Johnny Farrell was the son of Irish immigrants. He learned the game working as a caddie in the New York City suburb of Mamaroneck. Catherine Marie Theresa Alice Hush was the daughter of a wealthy engineer. A striking blonde, she learned the game as a girl, spending the summers at her family's club in nearby Old Greenwich, Connecticut.

By the time they met, in 1930, Johnny Farrell was an enormous star. In 1927, he had won a remarkable eight tournaments. His defeat of Bobby Jones—then the game's most dominant player—by a stroke in a dramatic thirty-six-hole playoff for the 1928 U.S. Open made headlines all around the world. The handsome Farrell, who was known as the best-dressed golfer of his era, had his picture in the society pages almost as often as it appeared in the sports section. The actress Fay Wray, for one, was a frequent companion.

Farrell was widely acclaimed for the accuracy of his iron play, and it paid off in a big way during a 1930 exhibition at Innis Arden Golf Club in Old Greenwich. As Farrell studied his shot to one green, he noticed more than the pin placement. He noticed Kay Hush in the gallery. Farrell laid his approach shot at her feet and introduced himself. A year later, they were married.

As it turned out, Kay had actually set her eyes on Farrell some months before the Innis Arden exhibition. One night she had been at the theater in New York with one Robert F. Wagner, the son of a United States senator who would go on to become mayor of New York. As she paged through her playbill, she saw an ad for Lucky Strike cigarettes. The man in the ad was Johnny Farrell, the famous golfer. So was the man seated next to her.

After they married, Farrell eventually gave up the Tour and settled down for a thirty-eight-year run as the head professional at Baltusrol Golf Club. He and Kay had five kids. Two sons, Billy and Jimmy, became respected players and club professionals. One of Billy's sons, Bobby, followed in the family business, serving as one of his father's assistant professionals at The Stanwich Club in Greenwich, Connecticut.

Johnny Farrell died in 1988 at age eighty-seven. Kay died in 1997 at age eighty-six. It is a testimonial to their remarkable love story that her obituary in the *New York Times* ran for twenty-six inches.

In the early years of their marriage, before their children were born, Sam and Audrey Snead traveled together. It didn't take long for Sam to give his wife a valuable piece of advice.

"Audrey, if I come home with sand in my cuffs, don't ask me what I shot," Sam said.

Naturally, everyone remembers the first time they met their future mate. In Corey Pavin's case, though, it wasn't quite as romantic as it first appeared.

"I was in school at UCLA, and I noticed this really attractive girl kind of staring at me," Pavin remembers. "I thought that was really interesting, so I introduced myself to her. It turned out that she wasn't exactly staring at me. It was just that Shannon had forgotten her glasses and couldn't see just what—or who—she was looking at."

The landscape is littered with stories of spouses who simply couldn't fathom their loved one's passion for the game of golf. But from Pinehurst comes the story of the honeymooning couple who seemed like a match made in heaven: his lack of golf skill was exceeded only by his wife's all-but-total ignorance of the game.

After watching patiently as her new husband flailed at the ball without making even glancing contact, she sweetly asked a very reasonable question.

"Dear, this golf looks like wonderful exercise, but what's the little white ball for?"

Greg Norman's wife, Laura, was a flight attendant, and it was a case of love at first sight. Norman, seated in first class, pointed to her and said to a friend, "See that girl? I'm going to marry her one day."

Sure enough, they married, but early in their relationship there was much about golf that confused her. For example, one day she was watching him pound driver after driver on the practice tee after a round.

"Greg," she asked him later. "You hit a lot more clubs than just your driver. Why do you practice so much with that one?"

Years later, after he had finished second at the Masters, a writer asked Norman if it bothered him that he might never win a Green Jacket and attend the annual Champions' Dinner.

"Nope," Norman said. "In fact, last night I had dinner with a champion. Laura."

The wife of a young PGA Tour pro sat in the bleachers behind the practice tee and watched her husband grind away in the hot summer sun. Finally, the boredom—and the heat—got to be too much. She motioned for his caddie to come over.

"How much longer do you think he's going to be?" she asked.

"Until he gets it right," the caddie said.

"Oh God, can't he just stop when his hands begin to bleed?" she asked.

A prominent player and his wife had been struggling with their marriage for some time, and their fighting had taken a toll on both of them. After winning a tournament with a $1 million purse, the player made a gesture of reconciliation to his wife.

"Is there anything you'd like?" he asked her.

"A divorce would be nice," she replied.

"I wasn't thinking of anything quite that expensive."

When Dave Eichelberger married his wife, D.C., she decided to surprise him by taking up the game. She took lessons and practiced diligently. Finally, she got up enough confidence to ask him if they could go out on the course. On the first hole, she hit a wonderful drive, then proudly turned to her husband and asked what he thought.

"With that grip, I don't know whether you're holding a golf club or a ham sandwich," he replied.

The Walker Cup is, above everything else, a wonderful exercise in civility, sportsmanship, and goodwill. This is particularly true when it is played at a place like The Country Club, which has been the site of so much golf history.

The 1973 Walker Cup was played at The Country Club, and, sad to say, it had its moments of strife—although nothing having to do with anything that happened on the course.

It seems that a postmatch dinner was scheduled. Actually two, since there would be one for the men and another for the women. This was all well and good, until the women finished their dinner in one of the upstairs dining areas and decided it was time to leave. The problem was that none of the men were ready to stop drinking and telling stories and just generally being swept up in the spirit of the moment. To make matters worse, no one bothered to tell the men the women were ready to leave. And then, to add fuel to the fire, some poor, misguided soul locked the women in their dining room.

It's safe to say that the postdinner conversation had almost nothing to do with the quality of play or the American victory that day.

Tom Lehman, the 1996 British Open champion, is devoted to his wife, Melissa. Like good husbands everywhere he is more than willing to go along when his wife suggests that it might be time to spruce up the old wardrobe.

To a point.

One day they went to a clothing store and picked out some slacks they both liked. As he was having them tailored he asked how much the slacks cost.

"Are you kidding?" he said when he learned the answer. "We're out of here."

There used to be a player on the Tour—a pretty good player, too—who loved his wife and liked to take a drink every now and then. The problem was that his wife hated drinking in general, and his drinking in particular.

One time he was leaving the clubhouse after his round when he ran into a group of his friends having postround drinks in the bar. They talked him into staying for just one. Then another. And another. After a while, his wife showed up looking for him, and when she found him all hell broke loose.

She accused him of being drunk.

He denied it. And to prove it, he leaned forward from the barstool into a perfect handstand and began walking across the bar, down a flight of stairs, across the putting green, and down the first fairway—all to a standing ovation from his friends.

His wife was not impressed.

Mary, Queen of Scots, may have been the game's first true "golf widow," although it's clearly not what she had in mind. Just days after her husband's murder in 1587 she ended her period of mourning and took to the links. Her loyal subjects were not amused, and she was soon beheaded.

TIGER WOODS

When Tiger was a little kid he would call his father in the afternoon and ask if they could practice together when Earl finished work. His father did a very wise thing. He always paused before he said yes.

"I wanted him to know that it was something special," Earl Woods says. "I didn't want him to ever take it for granted."

Very early on, Earl Woods had an inkling that his son might become an exceptional golfer.

"When he was very little, he mimicked my swing," Earl Woods said. "In fact, he was a mirror image, since he swung left-handed. One day he stopped in midswing and hit the ball right-handed. I thought, 'Oh, my. I've got something special on my hands.'"

185

By the time he was fourteen, Tiger Woods was already a favorite in most of the tournaments he entered. That was certainly the case in 1990, when he entered the U.S. Junior Amateur Championship at the Lake Merced Golf and Country Club near San Francisco.

But Woods lost in the semifinals to Dennis Hillman. After the match, he was angry and frustrated—perhaps as only a kid can be. But the anger lasted for only a few moments, until he saw his father standing by the green. Tiger walked over and gave his father a hug.

"Dad," he said. "I really love you."

He would be back the next year to win the first of his three U.S. Juniors.

Tiger Woods's record-setting win at the 1997 Masters was dramatic on a variety of levels. Not the least of which was the fact that it marked the first time a non-Caucasian won this prestigious tournament played in the heart of the Old South.

When Woods entered the clubhouse for the traditional dinner honoring the new champion, the members stood and applauded. But more important—and poignant—was the other group of people who stood and showed their appreciation for his accomplishment: the mostly black waiters and kitchen staff, who basked in the reflected glow of all that Tiger Woods had accomplished that historic week.

After the Green Jacket ceremony, the interviews, and the official club dinner were behind him, Tiger Woods, his family, and a few friends gathered at the house he'd rented for the week. There, the champagne flowed—and probably some tears of joy as well. But finally, Tiger excused himself and stole away to the solitude of his bedroom. A short while later, his parents looked in on their young son and found him sound asleep, his newly won Green Jacket tucked safely in his arms.

BABE ZAHARIAS

It's been more than thirty years since Babe Zaharias died from cancer at age forty-five, but even now it's hard to put in perspective what a remarkable athlete she truly was. She won two gold medals and a silver medal in the track and field competition at the 1932 Olympics. She was an all-American basketball player, she was an expert swimmer, diver, and tennis player, and she played baseball, softball, and basketball professionally.

Then she took up golf.

Sportswriter Grantland Rice got her interested in the game in 1935. Less than a year later, she had won her first tournament. In 1946–47 she won seventeen amateur tournaments in a row, including the 1946 U.S. Women's Amateur and the 1947 British Ladies Amateur—the first time it was won by an American since it began in 1893.

She was a founding member of the LPGA and won thirty-one tournaments, including three U.S. Women's Opens. She also brought much-needed publicity and charisma to the LPGA, in part because of her fame as an athlete but also because of her willingness to travel the country playing exhibitions and giving clinics.

It was at an exhibition that a man asked her how she was able to hit the ball so far.

"Honey," she said. "I just loosen this damn girdle and let her rip."

The wire services picked up the quote, and the next day it made headlines across the country.

Not surprisingly, the Babe was a confident, even cocky, athlete. It's also no surprise that this didn't always sit well with her fellow golfers. For example, how thrilled would you be if you were sitting in the locker room before your round and the Babe walked in and asked—as she often did—"Which one of you girls is gonna finish second this week?"

INDEX